AN APOSTOLIC HANDBOOK

VOLUME ONE - GUIDANCE ON FAITH AND ORDER IN THE APOSTOLIC PASTORAL CONGRESS

AUTHOR: DOYÉ AGAMA

An environmentally friendly book printed and bound in England by www.printondemand-worldwide.com

This book is made entirely of chain-of-custody materials

http://www.fast-print.net/bookshop

AN APOSTOLIC HANDBOOK:
Volume One – Guidance on Faith and Order
in the Apostolic Pastoral Congress
Copyright © Doyé Agama 2015

All rights reserved

No part of this book may be reproduced in any form by photocopying
or any electronic or mechanical means, including information storage
or retrieval systems, without permission in writing from both the
copyright owner and the publisher of the book.

The right of Doyé Agama to be identified as the author of this work has
been asserted by him in accordance with the Copyright, Designs and
Patents Act 1988 and any subsequent amendments thereto.

All scripture references (unless otherwise indicated) are taken from the New
King James Verion ® Copyright © 1982 by Thomas Nelson. Used by
permission. All rights reserved.

A catalogue record for this book is available from the British Library

ISBN 978-178456-198-7

First published 2015 by
FASTPRINT PUBLISHING
Peterborough, England.

Contents

Preface 7
Introduction 9
Founder and Presiding Archbishop 15
Congress Statement of Faith 27
The Nicene Creed 35
Our Convergence Movement 39
    Where the APC Stands 47
Our Ecumenical Engagements 57
Collegiality and Apostolicity of Origins 63
Apostolicity in the APC 77
Apostolic Succession 89
    Apostles and Bishops 91
    Apostleship in the 21st Century 103
Marks of Apostleship 107
Our Lines of Apostolic Succession 127
Archbishop Doyé Agama's Consecration 135
Other Lines of Succession 138
    The Methodist Connection 144
    Deacons, Priests and Bishops 147
Ordination/ Consecration of APC Bishops 157
    The Episcopal Ministry 158
    The Process of Selection and Consecration 162
    Recording of the Consecration 165
    The Roles of the New Bishops 169
The Qualities of an APC Bishop 171
The Noble Communion and Holy Apostolic Order of St Hadrian of Canterbury 183
    Works of the Order: 184
    Membership and the Rule of the Order: 185
    The Chivalric Ranks of the Order: 187

Preface

- What does it mean to be Apostolic in the 21st Century?

- How can we renew our historic roots and seek greater local unity with other Christians while remaining authentic as Pentecostals?

- How can we be better at affecting the wider community and the issues that affect all the members of our community?

- What is our contribution to the wider unity of the church and to peace and justice in the world?

- How does our ethnicity, nationality and personal history help us unite the church and the wider community in Christ?

This book series addresses issues of Faith and Order and to some extent issues of life and work. The Congress believes in growing koinonia through working together, finding the common things that unite us as Christians and bringing our differing gifts into common purpose in proclaiming the Gospel of Christ in unity. The Congress seeks a more holistic approach with greater "integration" between aspects of faith and works. This series of books seeks to provide answers to a number questions about our doctrines and the application of our faith in formation of ministry and our continuing personal and professional development.

Volume ONE is more of theological and philosophical underpinnings, while Volume TWO is more of the practical outworking of our ministry. There are many overlaps and the division into these two sections is more of a convenience than a necessity.

Future volumes will explore other important areas and may revisit some of the current topics in greater depth with updated information.

We hope that you find food for thought, inspiration and action as you read...

Grace and Peace to You!

Archbishop Doyé Agama – March 2015

Introduction

Within these publications, we outline aspects of our Faith and Order, as well as our processes of ministry formation, and acceptance for ordination. We lay a great emphasis on reflective ministry practice as well as on continuing personal and professional development (CPPD). We offer structured and informal Post Graduate training for Clergy from the entry level to the Pastorate or Priesthood, through to the Episcopal offices of the Presiding Bishop or General Overseer, according to needs.

Our vision is that Priests, Bishops and other clergy are a gift to the whole church and to the whole community, and not just to a denomination. As such, our training includes aspects of ecumenical and governmental relations, as well as community development. We also have one of the very few Pentecostal Chivalric Orders in the World.

The main ranks of Priests in this Congress are Deacons, Priests and Bishops. Our training combines Practical Theology with career progression founded on covenant relationships, mentoring and apprenticeships; and as such, our training supplements the more traditional academic training of some other institutions. Our training is conducted through St Hadrian's College Manchester, England. St Hadrian's College is the "Training name of the APC". Our graduating candidates are generally ordained at a Eucharistic Service of Celebration, Ordination and Licensing during the Annual Congress, usually each October.

Students at St Hadrian's College receive a deeper appreciation of Apostolic teaching and traditions from the foundations of Christianity; and support to develop their own particular ministry articulation and Apostolic impartation, into a real contemporary relevance. We also offer them specific information about, and connection to Apostolic Continuity through authentic and verifiable "Spiritual Lineages" and heritages. For us though, such succession must also be rooted in the wider apostolicity of the church as a Christian community. Although we regard Apostolic Succession as a neither a pre-requisite of entry to heaven or for successful Christian ministry, we do regard it an honour to be counted in such lineage where this is verifiable, valid, and correctly set within the church.

In preparation for ordination and licensing, we support candidates to complete various specialized training courses in relevant areas of their ministry.

Principles of Ministry Formation in the APC

Ministry formation in the APC broadly incorporates the four traditional "pillars" of the historic churches. However most applicants for APC Membership will have had prior experience of theological study and practical ministry. Formation in the APC is therefore shorter (as little as 9 months to 1 year), and is focused with particular emphasis on specific practical aspects of contemporary ministry expression; to "fill in the gaps". Formation in the APC is therefore tailored to the individual requirements of the candidate in the following ways.

Human Formation: Facilitating sound family life and the life of the APC member as a part of a living

Christian Community (local church or other ministry), through conversation, study, mentoring and modelling

Spiritual Formation: Developing the Christian spirituality, of APC members through lectures, tutorials and other interactions towards improving their understanding of the vocation of priesthood, sacraments and liturgy

Intellectual Formation: Seminars, open conversations, readings, visitations and other discussions; as well as journaling for more reflective ministry, towards nurturing deeper personal, historical and doctrinal perspectives of Christian faith.

Pastoral Formation: Teaching, studying modelling leadership of the Christian Community, both in the local church (pastoral team) and through the wider dimensions of pastoral care in the community

Our members are also offered opportunities for strategic networking, participation in organized ecumenical interactions and also take part in city/nation-wide and international evangelistic or revival events. Additionally, they receive help in working on their personal profiles and ministry projections for at least the next two years.

Our training is Apostolic in the geographical, jurisdictional, historical and prophetic realms; crafting a contemporary Biblically Orthodox Christian Ministry. Our staff have been working for over 20 years to provide specialized training and continuing professional development for Christian Ministry & Missions; including Ordination & Ministerial Accreditation.

Founder and Presiding Archbishop

Born into an Anglican home in Southampton, England in 1956, Archbishop Doyé Teido Agama is a Christian leader in the United Kingdom, and internationally. He is Presiding Prelate and Executive Director of the Apostolic Pastoral Congress, with over fifteen thousand clergy across the globe. He has served as a leading figure in Churches Together in England; and Greater Manchester Churches Together (GMCT). He maintains a keen interest in African Diaspora and Black and multicultural affairs. He has deep links with Nigeria, Malawi, Ghana, India and Pakistan.

Archbishop Doyé Agama

The Apostolic Pastoral Congress (formerly called "Apostolic Pastoral Association"), is a collegiate collective of Pentecostal Bishops, Priests, Pastors and other clergy that was formally registered in England and Wales in 2007. The Congress is conservative in its theology, confessing the Apostles and Nicene Creeds, and has formally adopted the Anglican Book of Common Prayer (1662) and the 39 Articles of Religion (1563). Archbishop Doyé Agama was elected Presiding Bishop by a clear majority of the members in 2007. Records of that meeting and those decisions still exist.

Archbishop Doyé Agama has served as a Director and Trustee of England's national ecumenical instrument, Churches Together in England (CTE). He also served as Moderator of the Forum of CTE, from 2012 to 2015, and was selected to Chair of the September 2015 CTE Forum, with over three hundred delegates from CTE Member Churches, Intermediate Bodies, Co-ordinating Groups and Bodies in Association. He has also served as Chair of the Trustees of GMCT in England's North West.

Archbishop Agama has a particular interest in the Early Church Fathers, and the Christian church of the first millennium in the Atlantic Isles (the British Isles), as well as the early monastics here such as those in Ireland, at Whithorn (Candida Casa) (St Ninian) in Galloway, Scotland, at Iona, at Lindisfarne, and particularly the North African (Greek-Berber) scholar-monk St Hadrian of Canterbury. Archbishop Agama has published regarding the matter of how insights from these times can help us in our personal devotion and prayer life in the 21st century. He studied for the Executive MBA at Portsmouth University and for the Certificate in Orthodox Studies with the Institute for Orthodox Christian Studies (IOCS), Cambridge (which is a member of the Cambridge Theological Federation).

Calling to Christian Service

In 1968, during a Scripture Union meeting in Nigeria, Doyé Agama made a personal commitment to living as a Christian. A particular spiritual experience of the Living Christ in 1991, radically changed his Christian life. He engaged in preaching and evangelism. He worked as a pastoral assistant in several Pentecostal churches, including some of doubtful theological foundations, but God mercifully rescued and restored him.

Many of these experiences were however also formative, in that they helped broaden his Christian experience beyond that of his early Anglican upbringing, and introduced him to some charismatic aspects of church life.

In 1994, at the age of about 38, he was first ordained for Christian ministry by Rev Dr Stan Dekoven of

Ramona California, assisted by a number of Nigerian Pentecostal church leaders. This first ordination was not strictly historically canonical, but served as an encouragement to service.

Also in 1994, Rev Doyé Agama was confirmed as an Anglican Communicant by the late Bishop Samuel Onyuku Elenwo, at Port Harcourt.

He also served as an assistant regional administrator for Elim Churches International (ECI) and as a regional secretary for evangelism under the Redeemed Christian Church of God (RCCG). On 27th November 2004, he was first consecrated bishop under the hand of Metropolitan Henry Paul Kontor.

Full details of Doyé Agama's journey to the historic archiepiscopate are given later in this book.

Archbishop Agama's Early Life

Born in England in the mid-1950s to Anglican parents of Nigerian origin, Doyé Agama was fostered very early as a baby to a white family. In the early 1960s, he rejoined his natural family in Nigeria, remaining there until the mid-1970s, where he experienced parts of the Nigerian Civil War. He later suffered from some post-traumatic stress.

Archbishop Agama's father was Frederick Abiye Agama. Frederick Agama was from Yenaka in the Yenagoa Local Government Area of what is now Bayelsa State, Nigeria. *He is seen below holding Archbishop Agama as a young baby.*

Frederick Agama holding the young Doyé Agama

Frederick Agama served the Anglican Church in Nigeria from the 1930s. He was a pioneer in the first Niger Delta Diocese, serving at various times as Diocesan Secretary and Treasurer. He was also a Lay Reader. He was one of the first Senior Staff Nigerians to be hired by Shell. He was instrumental in the creation of the Bayelsa State as a State within the Federal Republic. He became a Clan Chief or King, the Ogbotom Edede of the Epie-Atissa Clan in Bayelsa State.

Archbishop Agama's mother, Beatrice Oyete Agama (née Porbeni) is sometimes known as Chief Beatrice Agama or as Queen Beatrice Agama or as Her Royal Highness Mrs Beatrice Agama *(seen above, pushing*

Archbishop Agama as a young baby in a pram). She is a prominent Nigerian citizen. She has trained as a nurse in 1950s Britain, and worked as a nurse and midwife in Nigeria and United Kingdom. She has been active in philanthropic organizations, heading several such bodies and holding board memberships.

Queen Beatrice Agama has served on executive boards at State and Federal levels in Nigeria. She is patron of many clubs and organizations. She remains active in Christ Church Port Harcourt and other organizations, including the consultative forum for the Ijaw Elders and Leaders of thought. She is passionate about issues relating to the Ijaw peoples of the Niger Delta. She is a Justice of the Peace and a Member of the Order of the Federal Republic of Nigeria (MFR). Queen Beatrice Agama is also a horticulturalist and an ardent florist.

Her father was Chief Nelson Kemeninabokide Porbeni, the Etonkepua of Kabowei Kingdom in the Patini council area of Delta State and the Ododommedo of

Asideni also in Delta State, Nigeria. Chief Nelson Porbeni was one of the last of the Great Warri Chiefs.

Beatrice and Frederick arrived in England in 1953, to further their studies in higher education, Beatrice training in nursing and midwifery, and Frederick studying on a Colonial scholarship in the field of statistics and mathematics.

Archbishop Doyé was born during their stay in England. Beatrice and Frederick have six children: Ebiye, Doyé (Archbishop Agama), Diezani (Mrs Alison-Madueke), Osiyo, Timi and Winihin (Mrs Ayuli-Jemide). Frederick Agama died in January 2004, after 51 years of marriage.

Archbishop Agama and his wife the Reverend Helen Agama met in 1980 and married on 6th May 1982. They have five children and a number of grandchildren.

Secular Career and Interests

The young Doyé Agama returned to England after 1970. He first took employment as a teaching assistant, in 1973. From 1975 onwards he has been involved at various times in community development and regeneration projects and initiatives.

He became a telecommunications consultant, working in the oil industry and with central and local government and the emergency services. He attained a wide range of skills and experience, including professional management, consultancy and engineering qualifications. He is a fellow of the Institute of Consulting, and holds the Institute's highest qualification, CMC (certified management consultant). He has worked in consultancy roles with many organizations, especially in the charity and not-for-profit sector, also providing mentoring and leadership training. He has worked as a documentary film maker, an actor, a jazz musician, as well as in various educational and teaching roles.

Qualifications held include the following:

- BA Theology in church administration and development (1994, Ramona, Ca)
- Institute of Consulting, Fellow, Certified Management Consultant (2013)
- MA in Pastoral Counselling (1996, Ramona, Ca)
- "Microsoft" and "Cisco" Networking Technologies, (various certificates)

At the time of writing (2015) Archbishop Agama was studying for the Certificate in Orthodox Studies with the Institute for Orthodox Christian Studies (IOCS), Cambridge (which is a member of the Cambridge Theological Federation) in addition to the Executive MBA at Portsmouth University.

He also holds a number of technical training certificates garnered during his career.

Archbishop Doyé Agama has also studied with

- Cranfield University School of Management

- Windsor Leadership Trust, alumni of the "Experienced Strategic Leaders Programme", 2011

And various others

Leisure activities

Walking, visiting historic buildings, reading good books.

Chapter Reference

http://en.wikipedia.org/wiki/Doye_Agama

APC internal research by Rev Richard Norburn

Congress Statement of Faith

1. *We, being MEMBERS OF the APOSTOLIC PASTORAL CONGRESS affirm and confess the following Five Marks of Mission and Statement of Faith and Belief:*

2. Five Marks of Mission

2.1. The Apostolic Pastoral Congress, in all it does, is guided by these Five Marks of Mission.

2.1.1. To proclaim the news of the Kingdom of Jesus Christ the Saviour

2.1.2. To teach, baptise and nurture new Christian believers

2.1.3. To respond to human needs by loving service

2.1.4. To seek wherever possible to transform unjust structures of society

2.1.5. To strive to safeguard the integrity of creation, to sustain and renew the life of the earth

2.2. All these are as endorsed by the forum of Churches Together in England, 1997

3. The Full Statement of Faith & Belief

3.1. We believe the Holy Bible, as originally given, to be without error, the fully inspired and infallible Word of God and the supreme and final authority in all matters of faith and conduct.

3.2. We are therefore committed to believe and obey God's written, revealed, complete and authoritative Word; THE BIBLE.

3.3. We believe that the ONE TRUE GOD pre-exists eternally and operates and is expressed and manifested, as three persons; Father, Son and Holy Spirit *and that these three are one and the same God*, sovereign in creation, providence and redemption.

3.4. We believe Jesus Christ is the Son of God, the Word of God made flesh in history, as personal Saviour and Lord to each and every believer, and also as God's supreme revelation to humanity.

3.5. We believe in the true and proper deity of our Lord Jesus Christ, including:

- His virgin birth
- His real and complete humanity
- His sinless life
- His authoritative teaching
- His substitutionary and atoning sacrifice through His shed blood
- His bodily resurrection
- His ascension to the right hand of the Father
- His present and continuing, heavenly intercession
- His promise of a triumphant return, to fulfil the kingdom by total transformation of the created order.

3.6. We believe that repentance towards God and faith in the Lord Jesus Christ are the essential necessity for spiritual, mental and physical salvation; by which the sinner is pardoned and accepted as righteous in God's sight.

3.7. We believe that Baptism by full immersion (dipping once and in the name of the Father, Son and Holy Spirit) following profession of faith (by the candidate for Baptism) in the biblical Christ; is a sacrament of Christ. We can however accept similar baptisms done only in the Name of Jesus Christ as valid since Jesus the Son is one and the same God as the Father and the Holy Spirit.

3.8. We believe that justification is imputed to us by the grace of God, because of the atoning work of Jesus Christ and his resurrection; and is received by faith in Christ alone, with evidence proved by the Fruit of the Spirit and a holy life.

3.9. We believe that sanctification is an event (or events) where we enter by Christian faith and understanding into God's holiness by grace, through hearing and believing His Word (the Bible). It is also a lifelong process of increasing holiness through spiritual experience, learning to trust God in each and every circumstance of life; gradually partaking more and more of His divine nature through Christ, who has justified us to God. Entire sanctification is therefore our goal.

3.10. We believe in and seek the power of the Holy Spirit Baptism to live under the Lordship of Jesus Christ in expression and expectation of his glorious interventions and final victory.

3.11. We believe that the fruit of the Holy Spirit is *always* manifested in holy living and that tongues are only *one* possible sign of the presence of God's Spirit in the life of the believer.

3.12. We believe that various gifts of the Holy Spirit are given to all who believe in the biblical Jesus Christ as the Son of God and who therefore, are members of the Body of Christ.

3.13. We believe that the Lordship of Jesus Christ extends over; and has the authority to displace, all demonic powers of evil which can and do possess persons and pervade structures, societies, and the created order.

3.14. We seek to exercise and encourage servant leadership among all who believe in the biblical Jesus Christ as the Son of God and who therefore, are the People of God.

3.15. We seek to support member Churches to incarnate the Gospel of the Kingdom of God in their own situations, and in every sphere of society.

3.16. We affirm God's identification with poor, powerless, alienated and oppressed people in their situation. We believe in the power of the Gospel of Christ to liberate and positively transform not just the individual, but the society.

3.17. We seek to take a prophetic stance against racism and other forms of prejudice, people trafficking and all dominating and dehumanising schemes which entrench cycles of poverty in society.

3.18. We affirm the Biblical ideal of lifelong, heterosexual marriage as the basis of family life and as the Biblical teaching and the Biblical ideal in the building of human society.

3.19. We believe that Christians should seek out and actualise practical means of assisting in the comprehensive development of the community in which God has placed them.

3.20. We therefore seek to build partnerships and fellowships, whereby and wherein the gifts and fruits of Holy Spirit may be given by God and received among us all; for our fuller enrichment and correction; across the boundaries and forces that hitherto divided the unity of Christ's mission. *(Updated, September 2013)*

The Nicene Creed

(Excerpted from "Ancient Prayers for Today", By Doyé Agama, 2011)

The Nicene Creed is much more recent than the Apostles Creed (above). While ancient church tradition puts beginnings of the Apostles Creed at shortly after the Day of Pentecost, the Nicene Creed was only adopted by the first Ecumenical Council in the city of Nicaea, in 325. Thus the Nicene Creed is known in Latin as Symbolum Nicaenum.

Like the Apostles' Creed, the Nicene Creed combines the functions of a "Statement of Faith or belief", with a teaching of church doctrine and is also used for catechetical teaching as well as in liturgical services.

Unlike the earlier Apostles, Creed, the Nicene Creed, has generated some theological disagreement between the major branches of the church. The main difference has arisen over the inclusion of the phrase "and (from) the Son" ("Filioque" in Latin). This phrase was added to the Nicene Creed by the Western branch of Christianity at the Third Council of Toledo in the year 589, in an attempt to emphasize the divinity of Christ.

Without this addition, the Creed only states that the Holy Spirit proceeds from the Father. Over the years, the "Filioque" phrase has brought considerable stress to East-West church relations, but most Eastern and Oriental Churches do not actually reject it. The do however insist that if it was not part of the original text, it should be recognised as an addition. We have included the "controversial" phrase in the version given here.

Today, the Nicene Creed is probably the most widespread Creed in Christianity and is highly recommended for use in both private devotions and public.

In this Congress as is the practice of many churches across the world, either the Apostles' or Nicene Creed may be used.

The Nicene Creed

We believe in one God, the Father, the Almighty, maker of heaven and earth, of all that is, seen and unseen. We believe in one LORD, Jesus Christ, the only Son of God, eternally begotten of the Father, God from God, Light from Light, true God from true God, begotten, not made, of one Being with the Father;

Through him all things were made for us and for our salvation: He came down from heaven, was incarnate from the Holy Spirit and the Virgin Mary and was made man. For our sake he was crucified under Pontius Pilate; he suffered death and was buried.

On the third day he rose again in accordance with the Scriptures; he ascended into heaven and is seated at the right hand of the Father. He will come again in glory to judge the living and the dead, and his kingdom will have no end.

We believe in the Holy Spirit, the LORD, the giver of life, who proceeds from the Father and the Son, who with the Father and the Son is worshipped and glorified, who has spoken through the prophets.

We believe in one holy universal and Apostolic Church. We acknowledge one baptism for the forgiveness of sins. We look for the resurrection of the dead, and the life of the world to come.

Amen.

Our Convergence Movement

What is now the APC began with a "call to the North", in 1999 from God to (then) Bishop Doyé Agama (who was working in London). Bishop Doyé felt commissioned to this work after prayer pilgrimages to St Ninian's Chapel in Galloway, Scotland, Lindisfarne (Holy Island), St Paul's Jarrow (Home of St Bede), Durham Cathedral and several other ancient Christian sites. From early beginnings in mentoring a handful of individual church leaders and working with several other organisations, the APC was formally launched in 2007.

Although the work is now national and international, we are "steeped" in the Christian history of the North of England and the term "Anglian" helps to identify our work with historic Northumbria. Anglia was a 6th century Anglo-Saxon (Germanic) kingdom in the area of Norfolk, Suffolk and parts of Cambridgeshire today. The term Anglia then became the Medieval and Late Latin name for England. Later the name was also used for all those Anglian dialects of Old and Middle English in the Midlands and the north of England including Northumbrian. We however do not claim links to any other group using the term "Anglian" in their title.

The APC also identifies strongly with the way great men and women of God were moved in the power of the Holy Spirit, in the early evangelisation of England, long before there was what we know today as the Anglican Church. We are not in communion with Canterbury, but we respect the history of the church in Europe where God has mainly called us to serve Him.

We have begun formal dialogue with the Roman Catholic Church, the Anglican Communion and less formally with the Coptic and Ethiopian Orthodox Churches. More of such "dialogues" will follow, with a view to deepening understanding and relationships of our churches and people; with the longer term hope of increasing our ability to do mission and proclaim the Gospel of Christ together.

The Apostolic Pastoral Congress (APC) belongs as a more recent entrant within the global phenomenon of the modern Convergence Movement, which was originally found among evangelical and charismatic churches in the 1970s; in the United State of America. Although the APC developed entirely independent of other convergence movements, there are similarities in the process of exploration and adoption of doctrinal, liturgical and sacramental practices from the ancient churches, but real differences positions on theology and praxis.

The pioneers of the 1970 Convergence Movement were mainly evangelicals such as Peter E. Gillquist (Campus for Christ), Robert E. Webber and Thomas Howard who began working with pastors theologians and academics. They also began some new networks of those who, like them were interested in the new movement. The groups and churches established by these innovators, began to introduce the ideas, practices and traditions of the ancient Church Fathers, mainly to the modern evangelicals.

The National Conference of Evangelicals for Historic Christianity gave the "The Chicago Call" in 1977. That conference issued a number of documents that are foundational to the modern convergence movement and included calling the evangelical churches back to Historic Roots and Continuity; Biblical Fidelity; Creedal Identity; Holistic Salvation; Sacramental Integrity; Spirituality; Church Authority; and Church Unity. For more on these aspects of the Chicago Call as outlined below, please see (Webber, R, & Bloesch, D., (Eds), 1978 Pages 11 - 16).

Historic Roots and Continuity – A recognition that evangelicalism or the active effort to win converts to Christ is not new to the "modern" church but has always existed as a strand within the continuity or heritage of Christianity.

Biblical Fidelity - A return to interpretations of scripture guided by the historical understandings of the church but still within the evangelical framework of the final authority of the Holy Bible

Creedal Identity - A return to confessing Christianity using the Creeds of the Historic Church. Recognising the validity and spirituality of the ancient Creeds as a basis for faith. A need to understand the Creeds as a basis for understanding scripture and adapting our witness to contemporary issues and situations.

Holistic Salvation - To go beyond doctrines of our personal, individualistic, otherworldly, spiritual salvation, to also include justice for the oppressed and the salvation of creation itself.

Sacramental Integrity - To recognise the unique activity of the Holy Spirit in baptism and the Lord's Supper (Eucharist) and to overcome the modern poverty of sacramental understanding through a return to the teaching of the Early Church Fathers and Reformers; especially the understanding that God operates sacramentally in and through His creation and in our daily living.

Spirituality - To return from excesses of undisciplined spirituality to one that is more authentic; freed from sin and freed from religiosity through the preaching of the Word in the power of the Holy Spirit. Drawing on the ancient spiritual disciplines of "prayer, meditation, silence, fasting, Bible study and spiritual diaries". Going beyond personal piety to identify with the suffering of the world, with an openness to the depth of all bible based Christian traditions, and.

Church Authority - to rediscover the expression of Christ's Lordship in the authority of the Church. To repent of the rush to "independence" in churches and ministries that results in a new "legalised indiscipline". To return to a godly framework of authority in submission to each other and duly appointed authority in the church. To rediscover the beauty of discipline and order in building the churches under the direction of the Holy Spirit.

Church Unity - to turn away from Evangelical sectarianism and to become a living visible testimony of Christ's great prayer for unity. To draw on church history and scripture revelation as a source of understanding the foundations of our unity. To recognise that God may be working in other churches than our own. To seek ecumenical agreement and understanding without compromise of the Gospel.

Several of the pioneers of the Convergence Movement were attracted to Anglicanism, as have a number of modern reformations in their explorations of the historic church. In this Congress we have found the classical Anglican Church to be an important bridge back to pre-reformation liturgy, vestment and sacramental practice linking the Western post reformation churches with their roots in both the Roman Catholic and the Orthodox Churches of antiquity. Convergence has also led many back into mainstream Orthodoxy. In this Congress we also rely deeply on Orthodoxy for enrichment of our spirituality and our prayer life, and our understanding of Sacraments; as well as the authenticity of the history and heritage of the church.

The Chicago call recognised the lack of historicity in evangelical church doctrine and invoked for a re-examination and recovery of our ancient Christian heritage as revealed by God through scripture. (Webber, R, & Bloesch, D., (Eds), 1978). However we may also note that the signatories of the original Chicago Call did not represent the diversity of ethnicity and praxis of the Evangelical churches in the USA and were largely a white middle class grouping at the inception.

A number of those churches using the term "convergence" in their name or tracing their origins to the Chicago Call movement have since grown towards the liberal side of modern church life with several advertising openly that they will accept almost anyone as a Christian Minister (for a fee). The APC however remains theologically, sacramentally and governmentally more conservative in comparison with some of the other convergence movements around the world.

Where the APC Stands

The APC forms a bridge between Liturgical/Sacramental historic churches, and the more modern emerging Evangelical and Charismatic churches seeking the unity that Jesus Christ prayed for in John Chapter 17. We stand in that gap promoting and working for the unity of the church and the unity of church and community. This Congress is also a convergence between the emergent African Diaspora in Europe and the older African Diaspora in the Caribbean and the Americas. This Congress has reached out to a number of African Diaspora Christian organisations such as the Joint College of African American Bishops and the preacher at our yearly conferences in England has usually come from the African-American or Afro-Caribbean Churches.

This Congress is also a confluence of unity between Black, White, Asian and other cultures and Ethnicities among Christians who have largely been divided along these lines. Our theology brings together historic theology, evangelical biblical emphasis and episcopal government, based on (but going beyond) the five-fold ministry model favoured by the modern independent churches. We bring the Evangelical personal conversion and the prominence of the continuing active presence of the Holy Spirit of Pentecostalism into the realm of historic Orthodoxy.

We recognise and incorporate the history of African Orthodox Christianity in our teaching and practice, particularly in the prayer life of the clergy. We teach the understanding of Eastern, Western and "Southern" Christianity to all our ordinands. We teach them the history of the Early Church in Africa, because we believe that until all the history of African Christianity is told, the history of Christianity itself has not been fully told. We also respect and teach that international interactions between parts of global Christianity, including between Africa and Europe have been happening since the earliest days of our faith.

We are global in our vision and believe that the gifts of the Holy Spirit are essential and integral to all evangelism and mission. We are liturgical in all sacramental worship with a strong focus on passionate bible centred preaching, but still allowing reasonable freedom for the charisma of the Holy Spirit even in Liturgical worship. Church meetings that do not include sacraments such as Bible Studies and prayer sessions are not required to be liturgical. Clergy are required to vest for liturgy but free to dress in their own way at other times.

In this Congress, social action is no substitute for personal holiness but rather both are essential to building the kingdom of God. Our ecclesiology is incarnational, biblical, and reformational in a positive sense that is respectful of church history. It is also deeply and unashamedly spiritual. In worship, we aim to combine the rational and the expressive (emotional), the contemplative and the exuberant.

- We believe that Holy Spirit is drawing the church together healing the wounds of the Great schism which began in the 11th Century (that divided the Eastern and Western Churches) and the effects of the Reformation in the 16th Century (that divided the Western Churches).

- We are committed to the importance of the ancient sacraments of the church and to the centrality of the Holy Communion. We however may express the sacraments slightly differently in the modern setting of our churches.

- We are committed to studying and understanding the ancient churches, especially the prayer life of the ancient saints and the history of the church in the place of our call.

- We are committed to ecumenism as a necessary step on the road towards the increased unity of the church, but not as an end in itself and always as distinct from interfaith.

- We allow our member churches to have their own emphasis. Some are more modern Pentecostal. Others are more Evangelical. Still others are more high church liturgical and even Old Catholic in origins.

- We utilise visual aspects of worship especially in liturgical services, but are conservative in adoption of recent additions such as liturgical dance and loud rock music etc. Bishops however have a great degree of discretion within the overall ethos of the Congress, to determine the forms of worship in their areas.

The Apostolic Pastoral Congress is global, collegiate collective of Pentecostal Bishops, Priests, Pastors and other Clergy, headquartered in the United Kingdom. It provides links into the majority of European church life through our full membership of Churches Together in Britain and Ireland, Churches Together in England (CTE), Greater Manchester Churches Together (GMCT) etc., as well as our growing working relationship with the Church of England Province of York, and in particular the Diocese of Manchester; and other church bodies. Members and affiliates of the Congress will be expected to build similar links in the area where they are placed and will receive such support as the presidium is able to give them in achieving this.

The Apostolic Pastoral Congress grew out of real needs for authentic answers to issues in pastoral ministry. Starting with a handful of informal mentees, it was not long before we realized that what we were learning to apply in our lives and ministries was useful to others and the APC was born. We swiftly grew into a recognized part of the mainstream of church life in Europe.

In 2012 we took a collective decision to transition from our current formation as an association, to become the APOSTOLIC PASTORAL CONGRESS. The term Congress has been in use by many similar groups to ourselves and generally carries a much more dignified idea of leaders representing independent entities, agreeing to unite for certain common purposes.

The APC is Pentecostal in expression, but is also episcopal, historic, liturgical and sacramental, in the recognition that the Church can only be ONE both in its origins and its eventual destiny. We can therefore also lay claim to any parts of the ancient Christian heritage that are not in clear conflict with the Bible, for they are not the property of any one denomination.

Some of our vestments and practice might seem similar to those in Anglicanism, but these (for example the use of the cope and mitre) are part of the wider heritage of the entire church and are not the property of a particular denomination. However we began as a group of British Church Leaders, and in that sense, could also describe ourselves as Anglian rather than Anglican. The APC however accepts the 1662 (Anglican) Book of Common Prayer and the 39 Articles of Religion.

The chapters and topics here outline a few aspects the Apostolic Pastoral Congress's theology and praxis in a number of areas within our episcopal framework. As such, this series of chapters serves us internally as well as providing us a basis for engaging in aspects of the ecumenical hermeneutics necessary for the types of Faith and Order discussions that have already made significant progress between existing churches and denominations at national, international levels and at the World Council of Churches.

In seeking to answer the questions of the true nature of apostolicity in our ecclesiology, we must be willing to also answer the related questions of historicity, liturgy, sacraments, ordained ministry and others.

We must attempt to ask ourselves what it means to be church leaders within the APC, what do we have in common with the other church leaders and what differentiates us? Why do we do things the way that we do? How does our particular ecclesiology draw from and relate to the emergent churches and from the historic church? What are we saying to the nations, to our fellow Christians and perhaps even more importantly; to ourselves? This and related publications are intended to enhance our internal unity, but to also to further enable our place in the wider unity of the church.

Chapter Reference

Webber R, (Auth), Bloesch D (Auth) The Orthodox Evangelicals Paperback, 1978 Thomas Nelson Incorporated

Our Ecumenical Engagements

For us in the APC, ecumenism is not unity, but may be one of several necessary steps on the road to a form of unity between the churches which have yet to discern. In furthering our ecumenical engagement, the Congress is a member of:

- Greater Manchester Churches Together
- Churches Together in England
- Churches Together in Britain and Ireland
- The Evangelical Alliance

The Congress keeps good relationships with the Church of England (Anglican Communion) with both Archbishops of Canterbury and York, and with the Roman Catholic and Orthodox Churches, among others, according to 1Corinthians 12:3, and John 17:20-23 20

> *John 17:20-23 20 "I do not pray for these alone, but also for those who will believe in Me through their word; 21 that they all may*

be one, as You, Father, are in Me, and I in You; that they also may be one in Us, that the world may believe that You sent Me. 22 And the glory which You gave Me I have given them, that they may be one just as We are one: 23 I in them, and You in Me; that they may be made perfect in one, and that the world may know that You have sent Me, and have loved them as You have loved Me..

Meeting with Pope Benedict XVI

Meeting with Pope Theodoros II

The Congress keeps good relationships with a number of other Prelates and Primates including His Eminence, The Most Revd Nicholas Okoh of the Church of Nigeria (Anglican Communion).

The Apostolic Pastoral Congress which has headquarters in Manchester in the United Kingdom, has members in Europe, Africa, Asia, the Caribbean and the Americas. Archbishop Agama has ordained more than 150 Priests and 6 Bishops in England. The ordinations and consecrations are often held in Anglican Cathedrals and those he ordains and consecrates are widely accepted by the historic churches.

The picture above shows then Bishop, Doye Agama (1st seated from left) with the delegation of the Church of Nigeria to Manchester in the United Kingdom in 2011, which was led by the Anglican Primate of all Nigeria, Archbishop Nicholas Okoh. Seated next to Archbishop Okoh is Bishop Mark Davies of Middleton, representing the Diocese of Manchester

Archbishop Agama is also Abbot of the Noble Communion and Holy Apostolic Order of St Hadrian of Canterbury. The Order utilises an updated form of the ancient "Prayer of the Hours" as adapted and published by Archbishop Agama. The Order is Pentecostal in origins, but ecumenical in practice. Members must be in good standing in churches recognised by the Congress. One category of "honorary membership" is however reserved for those who are not required to keep to the rules of the order. The Grand Patron of the Order is Prince Ermias Sahle-Selassie Haile-Selassie, President of the Crown Council of Ethiopia and a grandson of the Emperor Haile Selassie (1892-1975).

Prince Ermias Haile Selassie

A number of distinguished personalities from across Africa and around the world are members of the Order of St Hadrian, among them His Excellency Dr Goodluck

Jonathan, former President of the Federal Republic of Nigeria.

With President Goodluck Jonathan

Collegiality and Apostolicity of Origins

In the early church there was not one clear and universal model or pattern of episcopacy. The role of the Bishop developed and emerged over time. In its earliest forms, each Presbyter or Priest was the overseer or episcopos of their local church (monoepiscopacy). They were elected to and installed in that oversight role by their fellow priests and with the agreement and participation of the congregation. However, there were other churches where the Overseer Priest had been taught by and ordained by the original Apostles of Christ, or by someone verifiably connected with them.

John Burkhard (2004) is of the view that the "classic" interpretation of apostolic succession simply as a chain of consecrations must be revised to allow a more complex and sophisticated view that includes apostolicity of origin, doctrine and church life; as well links of historic succession through ordination. If historically, apostolicity of origin refers to links between an existing church and an original "Mother Church" founded by one of the 12 Apostles, it is clear that similar patterns are found among the emerging churches, particularly those that were planted by a charismatic "founding apostle". Apostolicity of doctrine has been a claim of many modern Pentecostal churches and here we are no exception. *Sola Scriptura* is not the total absence of Tradition, but a system of excluding any tradition that we cannot directly relate to Scripture. Thus *Sola Scriptura* is our method of safeguarding against encroachment by any Tradition that could be considered (or become) contrary to Scripture.

Apostolicity of Origin

Pope Benedict XVI, writing as the former Joseph Cardinal Ratzinger in the book *Principles of Catholic Theology: Building Stones for a Fundamental Theology,* tr. Mary Frances McCarthy (Ignatius Press, 1987, Pp. 245-46) agrees with him; that every granting of "Apostolic Succession" must be contextualized in the "existential and traditional" life of the Church to be truly ecclesial.

> *First, the inadequacy of the older, and what had become the classic, interpretation of apostolic succession as an unbroken chain of valid episcopal ordinations has been largely modified as the principal way of understanding apostolicity. Moreover, the image of a chain of episcopal ordinations assuring the validity of ministry that this rather mechanical theory entailed has been largely abandoned. Catholic theologians who have expressed serious reservations as to the adequacy of this theory of apostolic succession include Yves Congar, Joseph Ratzinger, and Francis A. Sullivan, among many others (Burkhard, 2004 Page 39)*

For us in the APC, validity of apostolic succession requires more than mere linearity and must in seek to include episcopal collegiality, and the participation and apostolicity of the universal church. Every APC ordination is very much a community event, in which we seek to involve colleges of clergy, and civic and church leaders, as much as the members of local congregations.

In this Congress, we retain a deep respect for Apostolic Succession, but as Pastors whose Priesthood and every existence is bound up in the emerging churches and ministries that elect us, our office and position are intimately linked with the churches and communities that we serve. This is reflected in the processes of ordination and consecration in the APC. Every member must be based within a church and every Bishop must be elected and serve within a group of churches and/or a geographical area.

We are a clerical collegiate collective, and a representation of those church and ministry communities of which we are an integral part and lead. For us then, Apostolicity cannot (in praxis) be isolated from a wider ecclesiology. For us Apostolicity is fundamentally the presence of the Holy Spirit – the Spirit of the Apostles, giving life and power to the Word of God and to the Church of God through the Word of God. Thus the linear view of hierarchical succession is for us an honour, but only honourable as lived out in holiness among Gods people. There can be no isolated hierarchy that is distinct either from immediate congregations or the wider church.

Our historicity is rooted in Christ and His Apostles, but also in the Old Testament prophets from whom Christ and His Apostles are descended. Christ is the son of David. David is the Psalmist Prophet. The Psalms of David contain more prophecy than most other books of the Bible. Jesus is anointed by the Holy Spirit who spoke through the prophets. Jesus is a prophet as well and as much as He is the Saviour of the World. The testimony of Jesus is the Spirit of Prophecy. We believe that Jesus also "formally" receives the OT prophet's mantle at his baptism by John at the Jordan, when God especially commends His Son to us.

We however hold a higher view of church tradition than most of our Pentecostal brethren. Our view of scripture is less the intellectual wrestling match of Europe and more like the reverential and literalist approach to the Gospels in Orthodoxy, combined with the post-reformation low-view of church tradition. We speak of the heritage of the church rather than of tradition, and see this heritage as a treasure chest from which succeeding generations of Christians can return repeatedly, for information, and inspiration. Our view is that the elements of ancient Christian liturgy and sacraments present in Anglicanism, Roman Catholicism and other historic churches are not private property to them, but are the heritage of the universal church and wherever these do not conflict directly with our high view of Scripture, we are free to learn from and utilise this heritage in relevance to our generation.

For us Eph 4:11 is still operational, for all the offices listed will be in effect until a time that is still to come.

While we must make a clear distinction between the 12 original Apostles and others so named in the early Church, in scripture and in the ancient heritage of the church, apostleship in the broader sense is plainly not limited to the 12 senior Disciples of Christ. Jesus sent several groups (including the 12) out on missions, in His name and with His authority (Luke 9:1–6, Mark

6:6–13), Then there are the other seventy (or seventy two) disciples sent, who are also called Apostles by many Orthodox Churches in Luke 10:1-14). There are itinerant apostles in the early church, at least some of whom seem to be regarded also as prophets. In Revelation 2:2 and 2 Corinthians 11:13 we hear that there are false as well as true apostles travelling among the churches.

> *Revelation 2:2 "I know your works, your labor, your patience, and that you cannot bear those who are evil. And you have tested those who say they are apostles and are not, and have found them liars;*
>
> *2 Corinthians 11:13 For such are false apostles, deceitful workers, transforming themselves into apostles of Christ.*

The Apostle Paul himself is not one of the 12, but one born out of season.

> *1 Corinthians 15:8-10 "Then last of all He (the risen Lord Jesus) was seen by me also, as by one born out of due time. For I am the least of*

> *the apostles, who am not worthy to be called an apostle, because I persecuted the church of God. But by the grace of God I am what I am, and His grace toward me was not in vain; but I labored more abundantly than they all, yet not I, but the grace of God which was with me."*

In a lecture to the Apostolic Pastoral Association conference in London Deacon Belete Merid Afessa of the Ethiopian Tewahedo Orthodox Church (EOTC) mentioned some Saints regarded as Apostles in the EOTC, such as Saint Yared (AD 501 to AD 571), St. Teklehaimanot the Ethiopian Apostle (1192 to 1296) and St. Giorgis of the Gasicha (AD 1357-AD 1416), regarded as a saint and Apostle of the Ethiopian Orthodox Church with a feast day of July 14th.

Apostolic succession was also not the major issue for the Reformation, but rather the abuse of hierarchical office. Martin Luther did not start out to found or lead a new church movement, but rather to reform the Roman Catholic Church. His protest rather focused on issues around the practice of baptism and absolution, especially granting and sale of indulgences. His treatise titled "Disputation of Martin Luther on the Power and Efficacy of Indulgences," commonly known as The Ninety-Five Theses was a collection of intellectual arguments around the realignment of church practice with historic theology and tradition. Whether or not Father Martin Luther nailed his treatise to the door of the Castle Church of Wittenberg in the way he has been shown in drawings and paintings is not the point. He would probably have nailed them up somewhere, because that was the normal way that intellectual theology was published locally in those days; and not because he wanted to make a dramatic pronouncement.

The Ninety-Five Theses of Martin Luther are a dispute of the validity of granting and sale of indulgences, and not of the validity of the apostolicity of the church, or even of apostolic succession. The Ninety-Five Theses are easily found in the public domain including the Internet, and are available in print from a number of sources, such as the "Works of Martin Luther", (Jacobs, H & Spaeth, A, 2010).

For some, to be apostolic means following as closely as possible; the foundational teaching and witness of the Original Apostles. Others lay more emphasis on continuity of ancient church tradition and spiritual links to lineages of leadership.

Among the Pentecostals, there has also been the "Oneness Movement" or "Jesus Only" who reject "classic" Trinitarian doctrine.

For us in this Congress, there is much more to apostolicity and succession than the mere creation of and occupancy of episcopal offices and insignia.

Everything we do in admitting to Holy Orders is bound up in the life of the local churches and community, as our processes for consecration show. We hold to the Apostolic Orders of Bishops, Priests and Deacons deriving authority, not simply from secret or isolated elevations and ordinations however authentic; or even public ceremonium that attempts to mirror the liturgy of the ancient church; (our ordinations are sacramental with a Eucharist and follow the ancient formularies), but receiving a living legitimacy from the election and support of the congregations and wider communities they serve. Thus, the juridical cannot be excised from the contextual and the communion of the Holy Spirit, which includes not only those in our churches but all true believers everywhere. In this way also, we only recognise our Bishops as long as they remain collegiate with us in Christian fellowship and in good standing with biblical principles of healthy private and public life.

We identify with and respect the Apostolicity of origin for which credible historical evidence is put forward by several mainstream churches of their founding by one of the original Twelve Apostles. We lay some direct claim to this and also to other lines and to still others that are more tangential through lines of succession that we are still endeavouring to trace and fully verify.

We have also remained open to continue deepening our relationships with those of our partner churches and ecumenical friends as are willing to share this aspect of their apostolicity with us. Some of these dialogues however may not be revealed for now as we would not wish to embarrass our brethren before they are ready to be public with the content of our discussions.

We however hold to apostolicity of doctrine, through the Apostles and Nicene Creeds, a high view of Scripture, and our holding to sacramental and liturgical continuity, within the framework of our Pentecostal ecclesiology. Here too, our knowledge and expression in being broadened and deepened by certain ecumenical interactions which should still bear further fruit.

We are the means of many smaller churches and Christian groups accessing and becoming part of the mainstream of global church. Our Pentecostal doctrine and practice is aligned with the wider and universal church, and we truly believe that we are part of the communion of Saints, the resurrection of the body and the Life Everlasting; and that all apostolicity must be rooted in the life of the church.

We are developing our doctrine with deep respect for the historic teaching of the Church Fathers like Justin, Iranaeus and Tertullian, but also with understanding of the need to write our own history in contemporary relevance. For us, sound doctrine gives structure to our understanding of theology. Doctrine is not a means to restrict discussion or reflection on scripture, but to enable them flourish in a framework safe for both the new-believer and the seasoned theologian. For us, "Sola Scriptura" is not a doctrine in itself, but rather a framework or yardstick by which we may examine both doctrine and tradition in order avoid falling into error.

Apostolicity in the sense of God sending forth His Message begins in Genesis, when the Spirit of God comes forth to hover on the face of the waters.

Chapter Reference

Introductions and Notes Volume 2 Martin Luther, Henry Eyster Jacobs (Author), Adolph Spaeth (Author) Publisher: Nabu Press (9 Aug 2010) (reproduction of a book published before 1923).

Apostolicity in the APC

This Chapter addresses the issues of Apostolicity and the Church mainly from the viewpoint of the 21st Century "re-evangelisation of Europe".

The word Apostolic (or Apostolicity) is most commonly used of, or relating to an Apostle. The word has its roots in Middle English, from the Old English apostol and from Old French apostle. Both these in turn came from the Late Latin apostolus, derived from the Greek apostolos, meaning a messenger, from apostellein, to send off : apo-, apo- + stellein, to send. So the Apostle is a messenger or servant specially commissioned and sent by God.

The word Apostle is found 19 times in the New or Renewed Testament, while the plural for Apostles is found 60 times. Neither word is used in the OT. However, the two Hebrew words that are commonly translated apostle or "apostelen" (in the Greek translation of the OT known as the Septuagint) are shalach and halak. We can see examples of this in Isaiah 6:8 and in Genesis 12:1. Sometimes as in the case of Isaiah 6:8, the call of God has no name on it and God sends the one who is willing to surrender and answer His call. The call of Abraham, though specific to him was possibly a call that had been meant for Terah his father who left Ur for Canaan, but only made it to Haran.

> *Isaiah 6:8 (NKJV) Also I heard the voice of the Lord, saying: "Whom shall I send (shalach), and who will go (halak) for Us?" Then I said, "Here am I! Send (shalach) me."*

> *Genesis 12:1-4 (NKJV) Now the Lord had said to Abram: "Get out (halak) of your country, from your family and from your father's house, to a land that I will show you. 2 I will make you a great nation; I will bless you and make your name great; and you shall be a blessing. 3 I will bless those who bless you, and I will curse him who curses you; and in you all the families of the earth shall be blessed." 4 So Abram departed (halak) as the Lord had spoken to him, and Lot went (halak)*

with him. And Abram was seventy-five years old when he departed from Haran.

Could Abraham possibly be described as the first Apostle in the Bible? We will return to his life story several times in this series. On arrival in the land of promise, Abraham builds altars in the land without delay, and through this begins to claim it spiritually for God. Almost immediately, he has to fight for the land and rescue both Lot his nephew and the kings who claimed to rule in the land before Abraham came in. So Abrahams presence begins to affect the spirituality, politics and the economy of the land.

In the New (or Renewed Testament) an Apostle is usually of, relating to or contemporary with one of the original 12 Apostles chosen by Jesus Christ, or one of the early missionaries of the early church; or one of such, chosen to pioneer the Gospel in a country or region. In secular use, the term Apostle also covers those who strongly support or advocate a particular cause.

In each generation however, there are claims to apostolicity and even Apostleship in the church and by various individuals. The term Apostle has been used by several denominations to denote those having a particular rank in the organisation's structure. Particularly within the European context, the APC does not support the "consecration of Apostles", as we shall go on to explain.

We recognise that proving a complete historical chain of continuity back through Bishops and Popes to Christ is difficult even for the historic churches, but we still regard apostolic succession as one of the important disciplines of the church.

Apostleship in the Historic Western Churches

In classic Western Church terms, Apostolicity is doctrinally of or relating to a succession of spiritual authority from those 12 original Apostles. Anglicans, Roman Catholics, as well as Eastern and Oriental Orthodox, and some few others regard this authority to have been propagated by the continuous ordinations of bishops. From a Pentecostal viewpoint, we can however say that if this is so, it must also be by faith.

Historical denominations also regard this authority to be a requirement for recognition of ecclesiastical orders and for administration of sacraments to be valid. The Roman Catholic Church however regards Apostolicity as being of or relating to the Pope as the successor of Saint Peter, whom they regard as the Chief Apostle.

Viewed from our vantage point in the 21st century, some apostolic gifting or anointing is clearly foundational, having to do more with pioneering work in the geographical or theological sense, such as doctrinal correction that sparks widespread revival for example. Others are more of maintenance or continuation and are marked by strategic managerial gifting including administrative organisation. The former often emphasises validity by signs; while the latter may emphasise succession. Neither is mutually exclusive and aspects of both could be found in each generation or in the individual ministry.

The Twelve Apostles of Christ

There has been some argument about the names of the twelve original apostles. Most writers agree that there were twelve, and we now know that back then, many people had more than one name. One was the name their family called them. Another could their general public name such as the son of such-and-such. They might have another Greek name to use with the authorities and so on. Some people in Bible days had nicknames based on their profession or their appearance or behavior. Jesus also renamed some of them.

The first 12 Apostles were all Jews and sent originally to the Jews. Mark 16:15-16 is qualified by Acts 1:8. Only at Pentecost were they truly empowered for global mission, and even then it seemed to be incremental; from Jerusalem to Judea, Samaria and eventually to the whole world (Acts 1:8). They were originally sent out in pairs, but later would work with others who were not always part of the original group of disciples (Mark 6:7, Luke 10:1).

> *Mark 6:7 (NKJV) And He called the twelve to Himself, and began to send them out two by two, and gave them power over unclean spirits.*
>
> *Luke 10:1(NKJV) After these things the Lord appointed seventy others also, and sent them two by two before His face into every city and place where He Himself was about to go.*

The lifetime of the first Christian Apostles is known as the Apostolic Age. The seats of their teaching and therefore the location of their authority; are still known today as the Apostolic Sees. The word 'see" comes from the Latin for seat, "sedes." The term Holy See comes from the Latin Sancta Sedes, or Holy Chair.

The 7 Ecumenical Councils & the 5 Ancient and Holy Sees

1. First Council of Nicaea (325)

2. First Council of Constantinople (381)
3. Council of Ephesus (431)
4. Council of Chalcedon (451)
5. Second Council of Constantinople (553)
6. Third Council of Constantinople (680)
7. Second Council of Nicaea (787)

Chalcedon was a city of Bithynia which is now a suburb of Istanbul in Turkey. The Council of Chalcedon met there from October 8 to November 1, 451. This Council was noted for disagreements over the nature of Christ. The decisions of this Council are not accepted by the Oriental Orthodox of Egypt, Ethiopia, Syria, Armenia, and the Assyrian Church of the East. The controversy over "Monophysitism" has now diminished somewhat, and the terms "Miaphysite" and "Miaphysitism" are now sometimes used as being more neutral.

In 451, the Ecumenical Council of Chalcedon also extended the title of Patriarch to the titulars of the five Great Sees of Rome, Constantinople (or Byzantium), Alexandria, Antioch and Jerusalem.

These were the five major centres or sees of the early Christian Church. These five sees are also commonly known today as the Apostolic Sees because they were said to have been founded by the first Apostles.

- Rome (by St Peter)
- Constantinople (or Byzantium) (by St Andrew)
- Alexandria (Egypt) (by St Mark)
- Antioch (by St Peter)
- Jerusalem (by St James)

There have also been some arguments over the Apostolic founding of Constantinople (built by Emperor Constantine on the site of ancient Byzantium) and the way in which that city then took precedence in order of rank above the See of Alexandria; which had always been second only to Rome. However, both church tradition and historical evidence point to the ministry of St Andrew in this region and there is some evidence that St Andrew did appoint Stachys the first Bishop of Byzantium in AD 38. This could be the same person Paul calls "dear" in Romans 16:9. However the position given to Alexandria below Constantinople is still a cause of some friction.

While there were other churches claiming Apostolic founding, these five (Rome, Constantinople, Alexandria, Antioch and Jerusalem) became (over time) the major seats of church authority for both ecclesiastical and political reasons.

These five sees (with Rome in the West and the rest in the East) were the basis for the Pentarchy or the way in which early Christian Orthodoxy was originally structured as five major groupings (of mainly independent or autocephalous churches), with each grouping headed by an Ecumenical Patriarch based at one of these Sees. Autocephaly meaning self-headed is drawn from the Greek term autokephalos and refers to churches who are independent of external Patriarchal and/or Episcopal control.

Nine other sees who could claim an Apostolic foundation and therefore the title of a Holy See are given below with their historic founding Apostles, and include:

- Athens, Greece (St Paul)
- Ephesus, Turkey (St John the Apostle)
- Seleucia-Ctesiphon, Iraq (St Thomas the Apostle, St Bartholomew the Apostle, and St Thaddeus of Edessa)
- Aquileia, Italy (St Mark the Evangelist)
- Philippi, Greece (St Paul)
- Thessaloniki, Greece (St Paul)[11]
- Corinth, Greece (St Paul)[12]
- Malta (St Paul)
- Paphos, Cyprus (St Barnabas and St Paul)

The first Four Ecumenical Councils are the most important to this Congress. We disagree though with the original language of "monophysitism" used at that Council and are pleased at the recent reconciliation between "Chalcedon" and "Non-Chalcedon" churches.

Chapter References

Burkhard, J. (Author), Apostolicity Then and Now: An Ecumenical Church in a Post-modern World, 2004, Michael Glazier Inc

Benedict XVI (Author) Principles of Catholic Theology: Building Stones for a Fundamental Theology, 2009, Ignatius Press

Apostolic Succession

Historical churches who follow Apostolic Orders hold certain doctrines regarding Apostolic Succession. These include the dogma that power and mission are transmitted or transferred successively down from the Lord Jesus Christ, through his Apostles by the sacrament of ordination. The Orthodox churches hold strongly to this doctrine. We have received a contribution from Deacon Belete Marid of the Ethiopian Orthodox Church to this teaching, for which we are very grateful.

Various forms of this canon (doctrines of Apostolic Succession) are also prevalent in European historical denominations such as the Roman Catholic and Anglican. Many other churches lost these types of concepts during the Protestant Reformation which initially lasted from about 1517 to 1648. These ideas however survived in several churches (notably in the Anglican Communion) and in some cases may have been kept in secret by others.

Some newer churches also believe in transference of a special anointing given by the Lord to the original Apostle of the church. These modern Apostolic orders however tend not to include a historical link to the original Apostles in the same way that the older churches do.

In many cases these newer churches do also attempt a return to what they consider to be the teaching of the original Apostles. The classical Historic Church teaching on this subject is that ordination within Apostolic succession puts each "spiritual generation" in touch with a flow of the sacred power of Christ, which alone enables true servant kingship, in continuation of the Apostolic mission of the Church.

Those of this school of thought would point to an early example of this process in the ordination of the first Bishops such as Timothy and Titus, who in turn were ordained by the original Apostles, and who had experienced a special call and commission from the Messiah himself. The lines of succession are traced from these early Bishops ordained by the Apostles through those whom they ordained.

As we have noted, we can find similar doctrines in many newer reformations who trace their beginnings to the original "commissioning" of their founder by God. However, some theologians claim that even the classical doctrine of Apostolic Succession is flawed because of some historic problems in tracing parts of the line back to the Apostles.

Apostles and Bishops

No one could fail to observe the recent proliferation of Bishops, Prophets and Apostles in many churches, including the Pentecostals. It is important to have clear or proper understanding of offices and functions. This Congress does not ordain or consecrate people as Apostle or Prophet. For us the Apostle is an anointing in the church and in some cases a gift to the church. The Bishop is an office of oversight within the church. In the classic Western model, the Bishops are the inheritors of the original Apostles who themselves are inheritors of both the OT Priestly and Prophetic lineages that converge in and through Christ.

> *Ephesians 2:19-20 (NKJV) Now, therefore, you are no longer strangers and foreigners, but fellow citizens with the saints and members of the household of God, 20 having been built on the foundation of the apostles and prophets, Jesus Christ Himself being the chief cornerstone,*

The APC interpretation or teaching on this passage is that the Old Testament Prophets are the spiritual parents of the Apostles, while the Apostles are the spiritual parents of the Bishops and the Bishops in turn are now the spiritual parents of the Priests or Presbyters and all others in Pastoral roles in the churches. None of these are anything without salvation through faith in Jesus Christ and the present Help of the Holy Spirit.

After all arguments about the lineages recorded in the Gospel accounts, it is clear that Jesus Christ had claim to both the Kingly line of David and to the Adamic Priesthood of Melchizedek. David, like Melchizedek was a King who also officiated in the ancient intercessory role of the Patriarchs stretching back to Adam. Christ may also have had claim to the Levitical line, probably through intermarriage between tribes. The evidence for the Davidic lineage and the Adamic Priesthood is much stronger and seems to have bypassed the "curse of Jeconiah" (Jeremiah 22:24-30).

John the Baptist stands in both the Old Testament Prophetic Office and is at the same time the son of a functioning Levitical Priest called Zachariah (St Zecharias). St Luke tells us that during the reign of king Herod, the lot for offering incense in the temple had fallen to a priest named Zacharias, of the course (or order) of Abia (or Abijah). Both Zecharias and his wife Elisabeth were of the priestly family of Aaron and were considered blameless before God under the Old Testament Law (Luke 1:5–11).

> *Luke 1:5-11 There was in the days of Herod, the king of Judea, a certain priest named*

Zacharias, of the division of Abijah. His wife was of the daughters of Aaron, and her name was Elizabeth. 6 And they were both righteous before God, walking in all the commandments and ordinances of the Lord blameless. 7 But they had no child, because Elizabeth was barren, and they were both well advanced in years. 8 So it was, that while he was serving as priest before God in the order of his division, 9 according to the custom of the priesthood, his lot fell to burn incense when he went into the temple of the Lord. 10 And the whole multitude of the people was praying outside at the hour of incense. 11 Then an angel of the Lord appeared to him, standing on the right side of the altar of incense.

At that time, the duties at the temple in Jerusalem rotated between each of the family teams or orders appointed by King David (1st Chronicles 24:1–19).

1 Chronicles 24:1-19 Now these are the divisions of the sons of Aaron. The sons of Aaron were Nadab, Abihu, Eleazar, and Ithamar. 2 And Nadab and Abihu died before their father, and had no children; therefore Eleazar and Ithamar ministered as priests. 3 Then David with Zadok of the sons of Eleazar, and Ahimelech of the sons of Ithamar, divided them according to the schedule of their service. 4 There were more leaders found of the sons of Eleazar than of the sons of Ithamar, and thus they were divided. Among the sons of Eleazar were sixteen heads of their fathers' houses, and eight heads of their fathers' houses among the sons of Ithamar. 5 Thus they were divided by lot, one group as another, for there were officials of the sanctuary and officials of the house of God, from the sons of Eleazar and from the sons of Ithamar. 6 And the scribe, Shemaiah the son of Nethanel, one of the Levites, wrote them down before the king, the leaders, Zadok the *priest, Ahimelech the son of Abiathar, and the heads of the fathers' houses of the priests and Levites, one father's house taken for Eleazar and one for Ithamar. 7 Now the first lot fell to Jehoiarib, the second to Jedaiah, 8 the third to Harim, the fourth to Seorim, 9 the fifth to Malchijah, the sixth to Mijamin, 10 the seventh to Hakkoz, **the eighth to Abijah**, 11 the ninth to Jeshua, the tenth to Shecaniah, 12 the eleventh to Eliashib, the twelfth to Jakim, 13 the thirteenth to Huppah, the fourteenth to Jeshebeab, 14 the fifteenth to Bilgah, the sixteenth to Immer, 15 the seventeenth to Hezir, the eighteenth to Happizzez, 16 the nineteenth to Pethahiah, the twentieth to Jehezekel, 17 the twenty-first to Jachin, the twenty-second to Gamul, 18 the twenty-third to Delaiah, the twenty-fourth to Maaziah. 19 This was the schedule of their service for coming into the house of the Lord according to their ordinance by the hand of*

> *Aaron their father, as the Lord God of Israel had commanded him.*

So Zechariah, father of John the Baptist, was descended from Abijah, who in turn was a descendant of Eleazar, who was Aaron's son (Exo 6:23 - 25, 28:1).

> *Exodus 6:23-25 Aaron took to himself Elisheba, daughter of Amminadab, sister of Nahshon, as wife; and she bore him Nadab, Abihu, Eleazar, and Ithamar. 24 And the sons of Korah were Assir, Elkanah, and Abiasaph. These are the families of the Korahites. 25 Eleazar, Aaron's son, took for himself one of the daughters of Putiel as wife; and she bore him Phinehas. These are the heads of the fathers' houses of the Levites according to their families.*

Abijah was one of the most Senior Priests at the time when King David reorganised the Priesthood. Ezra and Nehemiah seem to indicate that the order of Abijah were not among the original returnees from exile. The family of Zecharias had probably returned later (Ezra 2:36-39; Nehemiah 7:39-42; 12:1).

Jesus himself proclaimed John the Baptist "more than a prophet" (Matthew 11:8, Luke 7:26) and submitted to his baptism (Matthew 3:13-15). In this we can also see the Lord Jesus deliberately linking his ministry to that of John, who is the last OT prophet and who also happens to be a Levite! Was this perhaps a moment of spiritual reunion of the ancient Priesthood of the Patriarchs (Adam-Melichizedek), the Kohanen of Levi and the Prophetic mantle of John the Baptist. Scripture also declares Jesus Christ as our Great High Priest in Heaven (Hebrews 4:14-16 NKJV). Please see the section on Adam, Melchizedek and Levi in Volume Two, for a fuller exposition.

The first Apostles of Christ themselves functioned as Bishops in several places, including Rome. They functioned as the Prophets of the New Testament. They also appointed Bishops to succeed them, rather than Apostles. Bishops are therefore meant to be the Apostles and Prophets of our day, but this has perhaps been overshadowed by the emphasis on the Episcopate as a denominational office.

Scripturally, the office of the Bishop is not a calling to denomination but to the Church or the "Body of Christ". As such a Bishop is meant to act in the interest of the entire Church and not in a narrow denominational or sectarian interest. Historically, the office of the Bishop is a successor or inheritor of the Apostolic Mantle. Traditionally, the Bishop's office is occupied by a male candidate who is considered through Apostolic Succession to have an opportunity for a special governmental relationship with the Lord as a father to the Priests or Pastors.

Historically, a Bishop is usually the highest ranking cleric or priest in a given area and sometimes answers to a Senior Bishop (often known as an Archbishop). Bishops can be in charge of a Diocese but can also have other non-diocesan appointments. In some modern reformations however, the title of Bishop has often been replaced by that of Senior Pastor or General Overseer.

Increasingly today there are churches who have considered and adopted or adapted this traditionally male role for female candidates to the Episcopate. The APC accepts that females are called by God to have oversight, especially where males are abdicating their responsibilities to God as is very common today. Some of these kinds of issues can also be very sensitive and should be handled with prayer and wisdom. However, the APC would view ALL appointments to Episcopacy as requiring both a Divine calling and a recognised "administrative procedure" for legitimacy both within and beyond the church.

Please see our writing on Women in Christian Ministry for more on the role of women as leaders in this Congress. The Congress however accepts ordination of women Priests within its context, but still remains biblically conservative regarding homosexuality. The position of the Congress on that could be seen to coincide largely with Resolution 1.10 at the Thirteenth Lambeth Conference of 1998, especially and particularly with regard to active homosexuals entering Christian leadership or Holy Orders.

Consequently, the Congress does not ordain or receive into membership any leader who practices homosexuality, blesses same-sex unions or preaches or teaches this. The Congress view is that a modern Western Democracy should allow those who hold to a conservative religious stand as much respect as those who hold to opposite liberal views; within the law. Otherwise, the very principles of Democracy would thus be called into question. All churches within the Congress are encouraged to be "voluntary associations" of persons who have agreed to the Statement of faith which upholds (among other things) a biblical view of one male husband and one female wife for life.

Episcopal Apostolic Succession is variously believed to confer special anointing to be a shepherd and teacher on a Bishop, and he and the priests he ordains are thus in (and are transmitters of) an unbroken lineage of spiritual ancestry that goes back to the beginnings of the Christian faith.

For us in the Congress, Apostolic succession (which was not yet a formal doctrine in the very Early Church) is neither a requirement for entry to heaven or for successful ministry here on earth, but is an honour and often has implications for order within the church. However, in line with the majority of Western (and Eastern) churches, we do not appoint, ordain or consecrate Apostles; rather we expect our Bishops and indeed every member of the churches to operate in some measure of apostolic ministry according to their own faith and calling.

Historically, Bishops are the Overseers, the people who have the spiritual and administrative oversight of leadership among the churches. The Bishops are the "chief administrators", not only of the strategic management of the church, but also of the sacraments of the church. Sacraments are central to the life and work of this Congress.

A sacrament is an official and recognised symbol or religious act that is also believed to be the instrument of God's grace to give a particular blessing or favour to the one who receives it. Sacraments are also especially important in the role of the Bishop as the one who ordains/licenses ministers and presides at the special celebrations such as the Holy Communion or Lord's Supper or Eucharist. The Bishop also prayerfully delegates these sacramental duties to others in the jurisdiction.

We shall study the sacramental theology and practice of this Congress in more detail in Volume Two of these handbooks.

Apostleship in the 21st Century

There are a number of people in the Bible referred to as Apostles, apart from the 12 originally commissioned by the Lord. In Western church history, it has also been common to refer to certain pioneers as Apostles, for example St Patrick, Apostle to the Irish etc. Deacon Belete has lectured at St Hadrians's College about the concept of Apostles in the Ethiopian Orthodox

Tewahedo Church, where there are a number of Apostles recorded and revered in their history.

From the late 20th century however, we began to see an unprecedented proliferation of "Apostles" in diverse places and formats; and the Pentecostals not wanting to be left out, soon joined in this competition. The Syncretist White Garment Churches (AICs) had long been famous for exuberant and flamboyant titles like "Regional Apostle", "National Apostle", "Most Senior Apostle" etc. In the 1990s, we began to see signs that the Pentecostal and Charismatic movements were following close behind. For example, we had C. Peter Wagner's The New Apostolic Reformation, and Ed Silvoso's International Coalition of Apostles etc. Others soon followed what eventually appeared to be something of a bandwagon. Today of course, there are "Apostles" everywhere, in addition to the proliferation of "Bishops" and "Prophets".

The Congress is nothing to do with any of these "Apostolic Movements". While respecting and working with all who proclaim the Biblical Jesus Christ as Lord and Saviour, we believe that the efforts of the emerging churches at establishing Church Government is a sign that order is eventually returning to the house of God, even though some early efforts to restore such order could appear to be more of zeal, and not according to knowledge of the true heritage of the Church.

We believe that while there can be Apostles called and sent by God in any age, what we are mostly seeing are some signs of apostolic gifting and possibly even revival, which are being mistaken for Apostolic Calling or Office by certain groups and individuals. In the same way, we have all been witnesses to another recent great proliferation of "Prophets" here there and everywhere.

While many believers have some elements of prophetic gifting – mostly intermittently, very few indeed have been called to the office of a Prophet. If you attend these prophetic conferences, you will mostly hear words of knowledge and sometimes words of wisdom, but very few prophecies. Let the buyer beware!

What is needed though is not overall condemnation, but right teaching, mentoring and other support to enable those of such churches that are willing to achieve some measure of ecclesiological stability and parity with the historic churches without losing their "Pentecostal Fire". This should in fact now be a priority for ecumenism and for future church unity.

That is the major calling of this Apostolic Pastoral Congress, bringing back unity, order and strength to a divided church!

Marks of Apostleship

There is also a strong belief among many Evangelical and Pentecostal Christians that Ephesians 4:11 points to a continuation of five "offices" in the Church.

> *Ephesians 4:11 And He Himself gave some to be apostles, some prophets, some evangelists, and some pastors and teachers,*

There has been some discussion as to whether these five are "offices" or "major gifts" to the church according to the context of the passage. As such, some churches hold these to be offices and have corresponding titles, others only recognize the giftings in people. Many historic churches, including many evangelicals however hold to a cessationist view that these gifts (or offices) ceased after the original Apostolic Age.

Among the Pentecostals and Charismatics who believe that these gifts (or offices) have continued, it is quite common to encounter the additional belief that all these five gifts must be present in the ministry of an Apostolic Bishop. We accept this to be the case, but note that the emphasis of the gifts will usually differ from one person to another. However God has been calling and sending people from the beginning of history and he has never stopped doing this (Isa 52:7, Nah 1:15, Romans 10:14-15). Sometimes the people God calls, just do not fit into any category you try to put them!

> *Isaiah 52:7 How beautiful upon the mountains*
> *Are the feet of him who brings good news,*
> *Who proclaims peace,*
> *Who brings glad tidings of good things,*
> *Who proclaims salvation,*
> *Who says to Zion,*
> *"Your God reigns!"*
>
> *Nahum 1:15 Behold, on the mountains*
> *The feet of him who brings good tidings,*
> *Who proclaims peace!*
> *O Judah, keep your appointed feasts,*
> *Perform your vows.*
> *For the wicked one shall no more pass through you;*
> *He is utterly cut off.*

> *Romans 10:14-15 How then shall they call on Him in whom they have not believed? And how shall they believe in Him of whom they have not heard? And how shall they hear without a preacher? 15 And how shall they preach unless they are sent? As it is written: "How beautiful are the feet of those who preach the gospel of peace, Who bring glad tidings of good things!"*

So much attention has been paid to the attributes of anointing for signs, wonders and miracles as the marks of an Apostolic Bishop, but signs and wonders come in many different forms. The life work of a man like Dr Billy Graham is an example of this. We also see St Paul laid claim to the marks of an Apostle (2Cor 12:12) which included Signs, Wonders, Miracles and GREAT PERSEVERANCE (many people miss this last part).

> *2 Corinthians 12:12 Truly the signs of an apostle were accomplished among you with all perseverance, in signs and wonders and mighty deeds.*

St Paul also testified to having seen the Lord (1 Cor 9:1-2, 1 Cor 15:3-8). He claimed the fruit of his ministry (planting of the churches) as proof of his apostleship, along with visions from God.

> *1 Corinthians 9:1-2 Am I not an apostle? Am I not free? Have I not seen Jesus Christ our Lord? Are you not my work in the Lord? 2 If I am not an apostle to others, yet doubtless I am to you. For you are the seal of my apostleship in the Lord.*

> *1 Corinthians 15:3-8 For I delivered to you first of all that which I also received: that Christ died for our sins according to the Scriptures, 4 and that He was buried, and that He rose again the third day according to the Scriptures, 5 and that He was seen by Cephas, then by the twelve. 6 After that He was seen by over five hundred brethren at once, of whom the greater part remain to the present, but some have fallen asleep. 7 After that He was seen by James, then by all the*

> *apostles. 8 Then last of all He was seen by me also, as by one born out of due time.*

Because of the proposal by St Peter in Acts 1:15-22 that any one chosen to replace Judas Iscariot as an Apostle, must have been a witness with them to the resurrection of Jesus Christ. This interpretation does not perhaps fully account for the Apostolic calling of (Saul) Paul of Tarsus on the Damascus Road (Acts 9: 3-9, 22:6-21), and the experience of many others since then which all indicate that encounters with the Risen Christ can and do still happen.

> *Acts 9:3-9 As he journeyed he came near Damascus, and suddenly a light shone around him from heaven. 4 Then he fell to the ground, and heard a voice saying to him, "Saul, Saul, why are you persecuting Me?" 5 And he said, "Who are You, Lord?" Then the Lord said, "I am Jesus, whom you are persecuting. It is hard for you to kick against the goads." 6 So he, trembling and astonished, said, "Lord, what do You want me*

to do?" Then the Lord said to him, "Arise and go into the city, and you will be told what you must do." 7 And the men who journeyed with him stood speechless, hearing a voice but seeing no one. 8 Then Saul arose from the ground, and when his eyes were opened he saw no one. But they led him by the hand and brought him into Damascus. 9 And he was three days without sight, and neither ate nor drank.

Acts 22:6-21 "Now it happened, as I journeyed and came near Damascus at about noon, suddenly a great light from heaven shone around me. 7 And I fell to the ground and heard a voice saying to me, 'Saul, Saul, why are you persecuting Me?' 8 So I answered, 'Who are You, Lord?' And He said to me, 'I am Jesus of Nazareth, whom you are persecuting.' 9 "And those who were with me indeed saw the light and were afraid, but they did not hear the voice of Him who spoke to me. 10 So I said, 'What shall I do, Lord?' And the Lord said to me, 'Arise and go into Damascus, and there you will be told all things which are appointed for you to do.' 11 And since I could not see for the glory of that light, being led by the hand of those who were with me, I came into Damascus. 12 "Then a certain Ananias, a devout man according to the law, having a good testimony with all the Jews who dwelt there, 13 came to me; and he stood and said to me, 'Brother Saul, receive your sight.' And at that same hour I looked up at him. 14 Then he said, 'The God of our fathers has chosen you that you should know His will, and see the Just One, and hear the voice of His mouth. 15 For you will be His witness to all men of what you have seen and heard. 16 And now why are you waiting? Arise and be baptized, and wash away your sins, calling on the name of the Lord.' 17 "Now it happened, when I returned to Jerusalem and was praying in the temple, that

> *I was in a trance 18 and saw Him saying to me, 'Make haste and get out of Jerusalem quickly, for they will not receive your testimony concerning Me.' 19 So I said, 'Lord, they know that in every synagogue I imprisoned and beat those who believe on You. 20 And when the blood of Your martyr Stephen was shed, I also was standing by consenting to his death, and guarding the clothes of those who were killing him.' 21 Then He said to me, 'Depart, for I will send you far from here to the Gentiles.'"*

While in the APC, we generally accept this view of the Marks of an Apostle, there are however other aspects of Apostleship that have been less popular as examples. We shall look at some of these shortly.

We have seen that the term **apostle** means "one who is sent away", from (*apo*, "away from") + ("stello", "send"). We could translate this directly into modern English to mean an "emissary". The emissary is the carrier of a message from the one who sent them; in this case, the Gospel of the Kingdom. So every disciple of Christ can have some apostolic aspects to their life and ministry, since we are all sent to bring good news to others. For example, Evangelists and Missionaries often have an apostolic gift to do the work they are called to do, though they may not be called to occupy the office of an apostle.

Firstly then, the Apostle (or anyone with some kind of apostolic function) must be ready to humbly and obediently receive and the message that God wants to give. They must not change the message just to suit their own preferences, just for monetary gain or for those who will receive it.

Ephesians 4:11-12 (Matthew 10:1-2) tells us that it is Christ himself that must do the calling and the sending, and that the purpose is always for the equipping, serving and building of the body of Christ, who in turn serve God in the world. No one who destroys the House of God can lay claim to apostolicity.

> *Ephesians 4:11-12 (NKJV) And He Himself gave some to be apostles, some prophets,*

> *some evangelists, and some pastors and teachers, 12 for the equipping of the saints for the work of ministry, for the edifying of the body of Christ,*

Also, the one who receives the message must be willing to go wherever they are sent to deliver the message, not just to the most financially profitable or the most comfortable places. The first preachers to the church were the Apostles. When we remain true to the Apostolic Gospel in preaching to the church, such preaching can be regarded as an apostolic gift. There are also false apostles at work...

> *2 Corinthians 11:13-15 For such are false apostles, deceitful workers, transforming themselves into apostles of Christ. 14 And no wonder! For Satan himself transforms himself into an angel of light. 15 Therefore it is no great thing if his ministers also transform themselves into ministers of righteousness, whose end will be according to their works.*

Thirdly, all apostleship requires discipline that is first learned as a disciple. A disciple can therefore be promoted to a higher level of apostolic ministry, as happened to the early disciples. Saul of Tarsus became a believer and was almost instantly promoted to an Apostle, but he had to spend time with God in the desert learning discipleship (Gal 1:17). We also remember that Saul had spent his whole life prior to this in the study of the Bible and theology; culminating with "sitting at the feet" of Gamaliel, the great scholar.

Apostolic ministry lifts or carries the church as a foundation. The foundation is that part of the building that often remains hidden while carrying the weight. This can refer to foundational doctrine, but may also mean serving God in other humbler ways even unnoticed; without always looking for the limelight.

In Eph 2:19-20, Paul states that the Apostles and the Prophets are the foundation of the Church, with Christ as the chief cornerstone or capstone. We have already looked at the concept of linkage from the Bishops back to the Early Apostles and the OT Priesthood.

True Apostles acknowledge and learn from those whom God had placed before them in the land. There is often someone God had placed before you who may only be a "gatekeeper" but that "key" they hold is the means of your entry to destiny. Abraham who could have gloried in the promise of God and in his military victory, is humble enough to receive a blessing from the "old Apostle" Melchizedek. More on this in Vol Two.

> *Genesis 14:18-20 (NKJV) Then Melchizedek king of Salem brought out bread and wine; he was the priest of God Most High. 19 And he blessed him and said: "Blessed be Abram of God Most High, Possessor of heaven and earth; 20 And blessed be God Most High, Who has delivered your enemies into your hand." And he gave him a tithe of all.*

In Genesis 14:18-20 Melchizedek (Malki Tzedek) King of Salem brings out bread and wine, he prays a priestly blessing, showing that Abraham is now the ruling conqueror of the land:

- By the promise of God

- By defeating the invaders
- By saving the lives of the kings in the land

Your "spiritual parent" does not have to be "more anointed" than you in every area. They only need to have the specific anointing to give you the blessing you need. It does seem that Abraham may have had a slightly different insight into the nature of and possibilities of the relationship between the believer and God by faith than perhaps Melchizedek did.

Holy living is another mark of Apostleship. Abraham refuses to take from the spoils of the war, possibly because these were connected to idols. In Genesis Chapter 15 verse 1, we see that "After these things the Word of Jehovah came to Abram in a vision, saying, Fear not, Abram, I am your shield and your exceeding great reward" If we also read Genesis 18:20-33, we can see that Abraham is qualified to plead for Sodom because the King of that city owes Abraham his life.

The ministry of an Apostle does not only affect the church. Apostles also affect the economic and social life of people in the area of the call. Paul's travelling companions were attacked at Ephesus because Paul's preaching had affected the economy.

> *Acts 19:23-29 And about that time there arose a great commotion about the Way. 24 For a certain man named Demetrius, a silversmith, who made silver shrines of Diana, (Artemis) brought no small profit to the craftsmen. 25 He called them together with the workers of similar occupation, and said: "Men, you know that we have our prosperity by this trade. 26 Moreover you see and hear that not only at Ephesus, but throughout almost all Asia, this Paul has persuaded and turned away many people, saying that they are not gods which are made with hands. 27 So not only is this trade of ours in danger of falling into disrepute, but also the temple of the great goddess Diana may be despised and her magnificence destroyed, whom all Asia and the world worship." 28 Now when they heard this, they were full of wrath and cried out,*

> *saying, "Great is Diana of the Ephesians!" 29 So the whole city was filled with confusion, and rushed into the theater with one accord, having seized Gaius and Aristarchus, Macedonians, Paul's travel companions.*

During the Niger Delta Revival of 1908, the preaching of Garrick Sokari Marian Braide so affected the trade in gin and other alcohol being exported from Europe to West Africa, that he came under scrutiny by the UK Parliament and his ministry eventually ended after a number of controversial confrontations with the authorities.

The original Apostles were not "Lone rangers". They were submissive to church discipline and authority themselves, and they in turn established sound doctrine and order in the church, including teaching and preaching, prayer, as well as proper processes and qualifications for the selection of leaders. We see this in the instructions of St Paul to St Timothy. Unfortunately today, several of those claiming to be Apostles have become almost a law unto themselves.

For this Congress, Bishops are the carriers of the Apostolic Mantle in our days. However, apostolicity in its essence in every place and time; is the manifestation of the gifts of the Holy Spirit in the Church. Signs of apostolicity in the church are simply signs that God is calling and sending the church afresh in every age. Such signs of apostolicity will never be at variance with the Written Word of God – the Bible, and in particular; with the teaching of Jesus Christ the Saviour in the Bible. For example, the Holy Spirit is the discloser of the Glory of Christ, not a promoter of mere human personality and fleshly indulgence.

Apostolicity in this perspective is best understood as a stirring up by the Holy Spirit, manifested in different dimensions at various levels in the church. Some churches (and some in each church) may seem to have more or less of what is the visible manifestation of apostolicity "breaking forth". While many may have some form of apostolic manifestation in their life and ministry, very, very few if any in each generation could ever claim to be an "Apostle".

Understanding of Apostolicity is crucial to the foundations, building and future health of the church, as the church rediscovers her role as the authoritative representation of God on earth. These principles also have impacts on ecumenical relations and recognition of Holy Orders and other Sacraments across denominational boundaries.

Issues like concepts of Apostolic Succession, have particular importance in the heritage and legacy of the Church including validity of ordination. For example, in some places, if the Bishop who ordains has no claim to Apostolic succession in some form, those he ordains will also lack that recognition. This can be important in parts of the world where traditional doctrines of succession have informed the general view of who has an "authentic" ordination, and who does not.

There is today a new search for aspects of Church Orthodoxy that can strengthen the emerging order within the newer reformations, and increase the ability of various parts of the church to work together. Indeed as the Pentecostal Revival of the 20th Century continues to increasingly affect the historical churches in the Southern globe and also in the North, we can also see an increasing interest among the newer churches birthed out of this revival in their discovery of the historic treasures of their faith.

At a time when secularity and other forces threaten to further impinge on the freedom of our faith and religious thought, churches are finding more reasons to work practically together, beyond the dry ecumenical exchanges of yesteryears. As we participate in the end-time harvest, there is also the emerging of an exciting new or renewed focus on finding scriptural basis for agreement in faith and mission, rather than the often sharply divisive edges of doctrinal divergence.

The modern Evangelical Pentecostal or Charismatic minister, especially those who seek to contextualise ministries birthed outside of Europe into that Western context, are further enriched and empowered both by greater understanding of these ancient church doctrines, and by taking the best of what they offer to adapt into the growth and stability of the modern Apostolic Pastorate.

The Apostolic Pastoral Association offers ongoing professional development to all our members serving in pastoral roles. The training is to help you increase the Apostolic content of your ministry, specifically to enable your ministry in the Western societies and in relation to the Historic Church. In line with the Western European context in which we operate, we do not however appoint or consecrate Apostles, since the Bishops in this congress, are expected to function as the inheritors and successors of the Apostles.

Chapter References

Burkhard J., Apostolicity Then and Now: An Ecumenical Church in a Postmodern World, Collegeville, MN: Liturgical Press, 2004

Sullivan F., From Apostles to Bishops: The Development of the Episcopacy in the Early Church, Paulist Press 2001

Our Lines of Apostolic Succession

The Apostolic Pastoral Congress lays claim to a measure of Apostolic Succession through its founder Archbishop Agama. The Congress does not consider the succession requisite for Salvation, but does consider it a discipline and a privilege to be in the chain of historical succession. Many lines or streams of Apostolic Succession now converge in Archbishop Doyé Agama. One Anglican stream obviously came from the Church of Nigeria, Anglican Communion through Bishop Akamisoko (of the Diocese of Kubwa) who joined in laying hands on Archbishop Agama on 19th October 2013 at Southwark Cathedral.

The first lines of Greek Orthodox succession came to Archbishop Agama through the Old Calendar Churches, (via Metropolitan Kontor). Metropolitan Kontor himself had been consecrated in the Greek Orthodox tradition (Old Calendar) by Archbishop Maximos and Bishop Panagiotopolos in Athens, November 2003. *See pictures below.* (We have not been able to ascertain the second co-Consecrator.)

Bishop Henry Kontor became known as Metropolitan Henry Paul Kontor after the consecration. Archbishop Maximus conferred the Archbishopric of Global Orthodox Missions on Metropolitan Henry Paul in early April 2004.

A number of Bishops assisted Metropolitan Henry Paul Kontor in the consecration of Bishop Agama by the (then) Apostolic Congress of Great Britain, including (then) Bishop (now Archbishop) Kwaku Frimpong-Manson, (who was also consecrated by Metropolitan Kontor in 2002), Bishop Danny Bennett, of Shiloh United Church of Christ Apostolic Worldwide and others.

Prior to consecrating (then) Rev Doyé Agama, Metropolitan Kontor received and recognised him as a Priest in a short ceremony to address the canonical issues arising from his first ordination in 1994. While it has not been possible to fully verify all the lines of succession present at this consecration, Bishop Danny Bennet is successor to Archbishop Malachi Ramsay, who was the first Pentecostal Archbishop in the United Kingdom duly recognized by the historic churches.

More details on other Greek Orthodox lines of succession are given below. Another line of succession comes from the Patriarchy of the East through the

Syro-Chaldean Archdiocese of North America. This succession derives through Moran Mar Rowell Shimun XVIII (Shem'un XVIII Rubil) (sometimes cited as XX), patriarch of Selucia-Ctesiphon and Catholicos of the East (reigned 1860 to 1903).

The line of succession from Mar Rowell to Archbishop Agama is as follows: On 17 December 1862 Moran Mar Rowell Shimun XVIII consecrated Anthony Thondanatt (Mar Abdisho Antonius) who on 24 July 1899 consecrated Luis Mariano Soares (Mar Basilius) who on 30 November 1902 consecrated Ulric Vernon Herford (Mar Jacobus) who on 2 February 1925 consecrated William Stanley McBean Knight (Mar Paulos) who on 30 October 1931 consecrated Dr Hedley Coward Bartlett (Mar Hedley) who on 20 May 1945 consecrated [Hugh George de Willmott Newman] (Mar Georgius) who on 13 April 1952 consecrated Charles Dennis Boltwood who on 3 May 1959 consecrated John Marion Stanley (Mar Yokhannan) who on 31 October 1976 was a co-consecrator of Bertram Schlossberg (Mar Uzziah Bar Evyon) whose jurisdiction, in 1995, entered into Collegial fellowship with Bishop J. Delano Ellis and the jurisdiction led by Bishop Ellis (then called United Pentecostal Churches of Christ).

Robert Woodward Burgess (a bishop consecrated by Schlossberg, and acting under authority of a mandate issued by Schlossberg) imparted the Schlossberg-Burgess succession to the bishops of the United Pentecostal Churches of Christ, the organization from which Pentecostal Churches of Christ has emerged. Further, on 5 March 1969, Stanley received Bishop James Andrew Gaines (Mar Jacobus) into his jurisdiction. Archbishop Stanley subsequently elevated Gaines to archbishop. Gaines was chief consecrator on 31 October 1976 when (as stated above) Stanley assisted as consecrator at Schlossberg's consecration.

In January 2010, Bishop Agama was received into the House of Bishops of the Pentecostal Churches of Christ (USA), led by Archbishop Ellis, and was duly granted "apostolic succession" in that House, to which the official record and certification testifies.

Canonical Issues Resolved

The Apostolic Pastoral Congress House of Bishops Meeting for the Confirmation of the Election of The Right Reverend Doyé Agama as the Archbishop of the Congress and the Christian Way of Life Churches was duly constituted and held on Thursday 17th October 2013 at Southwark Cathedral, London, England. The confirmation was in three stages. First the House of Bishops received the report of the election during the previous AGM. The House then identified and questioned the Archbishop Elect. Finally, the House certified the Confirmation of the Election of The Right Reverend Doyé Agama as the Archbishop of the Apostolic Pastoral Congress and the Christian Way of Life Churches; before the clergy and congregation assembled.

Prior to his Archiepiscopal Consecration, a special vigil service was also held at on Thursday 17th October 2013, Southwark Cathedral, England, where (then) Bishop Agama publicly reaffirmed the vows of Priesthood and the previous Episcopal vows before the assembled clergy and guest laity. Bishop Woodson, Bishop Douglass and other Bishops present then laid hands on him including several Bishops from the Apostolic Congress, in deliberate reaffirmation and to some degree regularizing or superseding aspects of all his previous ordinations (1994) and consecration (2004).

This was done in part, to legalise any outstanding canonical issues from Archbishop Agama's previous ordinations and consecration.

These Bishops also questioned the Archbishop Elect on his candidacy. Some details of the Apostolic Succession of these Bishops and of Archbishop Agama, are given below.

Archbishop Doyé Agama's Consecration

When Bishop Agama was elevated to the status of Archbishop on 19 October 2013, during a ceremony in London, England, held at Southwark Cathedral. Archbishop Ellis again provided a "Consecration Mandate" which was read during the ceremony, and Archbishop Ellis sent an episcopal delegation from USA to London, England.

The delegation consisted of Bishop Darryl Woodson (leader of the delegation) and Bishop Benjamin Douglass; both of these being bishops in the Pentecostal Churches of Christ, Cleveland Ohio, USA and drawing their Apostolic Succession from Archbishop J. Delano Ellis II.

Bishop Benjamin Douglass was consecrated in August of 1999 by Archbishop J. Delano Ellis II, assisted by Bishop Carl Montgomery and Bishop James Lionel Chambers. Bishop Darryl Woodson was consecrated 29th June 2005 by Bishop Larry Trotter who himself was previously consecrated by Archbishop Ellis. Bishop Eric Garnes and Archbishop Ellis were also present along with Bishop Millicent Hunter and all laid their hands on Bishop Darryl Woodson in the Act of Consecration.

Before the Act of Consecration, Archbishop Elect Doyé Agama was presented to the people. Reverend Eric Scotland, Chancellor (Director of Administration and Finance) of the Congress and Minister of the Court, read the Authority of the Congress for the Consecration and requested the Consecrators to lay their hands on Bishop Doyé Agama and inaugurate him to the Office of Archbishop. The special consecration mandate from Archbishop Ellis carried by his delegation authorising the consecration to be so performed was then read out. The Congregation was questioned on their acceptance of the new Archbishop, who was asked to recite the Apostles Creed, before he was consecrated and given the Pallium granted to him by Archbishop J. Delano Ellis II. Details of the service of Consecration are in the service booklet. The role of Bishop Duke Akamisoko was deliberately given a "low profile" in that service booklet due to some tensions between the Anglican Churches of England and Nigeria at that time.

Bishop Woodson presided at the ceremony of elevation, as Chief Consecrator (representing Archbishop Ellis), and he was assisted by Bishop Douglass. The Rt. Rev Duke Akamisoko, Diocesan of the Kubwa Diocese, within the province of Abuja, in the Church of Nigeria - Anglican Communion also joined in laying hands on the Archbishop Agama at Southwark Cathedral. The Most Rev Justin Welby, Archbishop of Canterbury was also officially represented at the Consecration of Archbishop Agama by the Bishop of Woolwich, The Rt. Revd Dr Michael Ipgrave who also represented the Diocese of Southwark. Also present in the Anglican delegation was the retired Bishop of Manchester, Rt. Rev. Nigel McCulloch. A number of other Bishops from within and beyond the UK were also present and participated in the service, including Bishop David Chaney of Texas.

Other Lines of Succession

There are still other lines or streams of succession that could be cited. For example, one of the bishops in the chain of succession from the Syro-Chaldean tradition (the Rowell-Ellis chain) is Hugh George de Willmott Newman (Mar Georgius). Numerous lines or streams of succession converge in Newman, thus forming what is, in effect, an "ecumenical apostolic succession".

For example, one of the numerous lines of succession that could be cited as converging in Newman (and thus in Archbishop Agama) is a line via Gerardus Gul of the

"Old Catholic" Union of Utrecht. There is a path from Gul to Newman, via Johann Kowalski (consecrated by Gul on 5 October 1909) and Marc Marie Paul Fatome (consecrated by Kowalski on 4 September 1938). Kowalski perished in May 1942 in a Second World War camp, either Hartheim Castle or Dachau. *(NOTE: There is also a second or parallel path from Gul to Newman via Arnold Harris Mathew.)* Gul consecrated Mathew on 28 April 1908. There is a dispute or question over the validity of this particular consecration.

The dispute or question is over whether (in 1908) Mathew obtained consecration from Gul by giving Gul misleading information. A letter published in June 1908 exonerates Mathew. Mathew died in December 1919. Gul died in February 1920. In April 1920, the Union of Utrecht's "International Catholic Bishops' Conference" declared that Mathew had been in bad faith when he was consecrated by Gul in 1908). However, the Kowalski line stands independently of Mathew, and thus there is a succession from Gul without relying on Mathew at all.

A further example of the Anglican stream, is that there is a line of succession to Archbishop Agama via Newman from Church of England Archbishops of Canterbury (and therefore stretching back in English history at least as far back as St Augustine of Canterbury (who arrived at Canterbury in 597). The line from Archbishops of Canterbury flows via Scottish bishops and then North American bishops and Bishops of the Reformed Episcopal Church in North America.

Further, some of the other bishops in the Rowell-Ellis chain held other consecrations. One such example is a line of succession from Archbishop Makarios (Makarios III) (lived 1913-1977) (Church of Cyprus). The Church of Cyprus is an autocephalous Greek church within the Orthodox tradition, part of the Eastern Orthodox Church and in full communion with the Ecumenical Patriarch of Constantinople.

Makarios was President of Cyprus from 1960 until his sudden death in 1977 (except for a short period between July and December 1974 during which Makarios was exiled following a military coup). For much of the third quarter of the 20th century, Makarios III was a prominent figure in world news.

The line of succession from Makarios III to Archbishop Agama is as follows: Makarios III (who lived 1913-1977) consecrated Theoklitos Kantaris (Greek Orthodox archdiocese of New York (Old Calendar)) who on 30 March 1965 elevated Walter Myron Propheta to the status of archbishop who on 30 May 1965 consecrated James Andrew Gaines (Mar Jacobus) who on 31 October 1976 consecrated Bertram Schlossberg (Mar Uzziah Ben Evyon) whose jurisdiction in 1995 entered into collegial fellowship with Bishop J. Delano Ellis and the jurisdiction led by Bishop Ellis (then called United Pentecostal Churches of Christ). In 2010, Archbishop Agama was received into the House of Bishops of Pentecostal Churches of Christ (evolved from United Pentecostal churches of Christ) and was granted apostolic succession in that House. This was further reinforced on 19 October 2013 at a ceremony of elevation to Archbishop in that two Pentecostal Churches of Christ bishops (Bishop Darryl Woodson and Bishop Benjamin Douglass) participated as co-consecrators and they were acting under a mandate issued by Archbishop Ellis.

Russian/Ukrainian Orthodox lines also converge in Archbishop Agama from Gaines who (in 1965) had been consecrated in that tradition. A Slavonic Orthodox line of succession comes in via William Andrew Prazsky and Anthony Prazsky who in 1976 participated as co-consecrators in Schlossberg's consecration. This Slavonic succession comes via Gregorious IV (Haddad) (reigned 1906-1928), Melkite Greek Catholic patriarch, who in 1913 consecrated Metropolitan Archbishop Dionisiy Valedynsky who in 1932 consecrated Metropolitan Archbishop Poukarp Sikorsky who in 1942 consecrated Metropolitan Archbishop Nikanor Abramovych who also in 1942 consecrated Metropolitan Archbishop Hryhoriy Ohiychuk (Metropolitan Archbishop of the Patriarchal Throne of Kiev and All Russia-Ukraine in Exile) who in

1969 consecrated Walter Andrew Prazsky and Anthony Prazsky.

In 2008, Bishop (as he then was) Agama and his wife were accorded a special laying-on of hands during a chapel session, by the Executive Board of the Joint College of African-American Pentecostal Bishops, an Episcopal College led by Archbishop J. Delano Ellis.

Among those who laid hands on (then Bishop and Rev (Mrs) Agama were Bishop Alfred Owens, Bishop David Copeland, Bishop Clifford Frazier, Bishop Jonathan Alvarado, Bishop George Seabright, Bishop Maureen Davies and others. Archbishop Agama previously held membership in the Joint College.

Joint College of Bishops 2008

The Methodist Connection

Another *less substantiated* line of succession comes to Archbishop Doyé Agama through Wesleyan/Methodist tradition, via John Wesley, Thomas Coke (1747-1814) and Francis Asbury (1745-1816) and two hundred years of Methodism in USA to Carl Edwards Williams and Reuben Timothy Jones who on 17 April 1970 consecrated J. Delano Ellis and thereby passed on their succession to the House of Bishops of the Pentecostal Churches of Christ. Williams and Jones were Bishops of the Church of God in Christ. Both of them were possessors of Holy Orders from the Methodist Episcopal Church USA, Jones having been ordained by Bishop Frederick Pierce Corson, president of the World Methodist Conference.

The question as to whether the succession through Wesley, Coke and Asbury is an episcopal succession is a moot point. Wesley was a Church of England clergyman, but he was not a Church of England bishop. Many hold that Wesley was secretly consecrated a bishop in 1763 by Erasmus of Arcadia when Erasmus was visiting London but that Wesley could not openly announce his episcopal consecration owing to the Praemunire Act of 1393. Erasmus of Arcadia was the Greek Orthodox bishop of Arcadia in Crete, a jurisdiction under the patriarch of Smyrna. In 1784, Wesley ordained Coke as superintendent of the Methodists in the United States. Coke, however, was already an ordained Church of England clergyman prior to this ceremony. For more information, see the wikipage on John Wesley.

Further, a book titled "The Bishopric - a handbook on creating episcopacy in the African-American church" (2003) by J. Delano Ellis does not directly indicate that Bishops Williams and Jones carried succession as bishops from the Methodist Episcopal Church. Archbishop Ellis states simply that Williams and Jones were Church of God in Christ bishops and that they possessed "Holy Orders" from the Methodist Episcopal Church.

This Methodist connection is still important to the history of the APC given the links between the early Methodist Church, the Holiness Movement and the emergence of Pentecostalism from which the convergence groups like the APC have in turn developed. While Methodism may not provide the classic form of Apostolic Succession, the lineage back to John Wesley is certainly cherished by this Congress.

Chapter References

For the substance of this chapter (and other parts of these books), we are indebted to Archbishop J. Delano Ellis, for "The Bishopric, A Handbook on Creating Episcopacy in the African-American Pentecostal Church, Trafford Publishing, 2003"

http://en.wikipedia.org/wiki/Doye_Agama

The Rev Richard Norburn also contributed to internal APC research

Deacons, Priests and Bishops

Our doctrine of Priesthood in this Congress includes a spiritual lineage to Christ through collegiate Apostolic succession, as well as a doctrine of reunification of the Adamic King-Priesthood of the Patriarchs (Order of Melchizedek) with the Levitical and the Old Testament prophetic office in Jesus Christ our Saviour. Please read Volume Two for a fuller exposition on the Sacraments, including Priesthood. The main ranks of Priesthood in this Congress are Deacons, Priests and Bishops. Much of what we will say regarding Deacons applies also to Priests and Bishops and vice-versa.

Deacons (Greek Diokonos) = a Ministry of Christian service. Deacons are servants, messengers or attendants. They may also be appointed to other official service in the church *(Blackwell Dictionary of Eastern Christianity 2000, Page 157)*.

The Septuagint (from the Latin septuaginta or seventy), is the primary or authoritative Greek translation of the Hebrew Bible into Koine (Biblical) Greek. This is the Greek Old Testament version most frequently quoted by New Testament writers, especially the Apostle Paul. The Septuagint translated the Hebrew "shawrath" (minister, servant, service) with variants on Diakonos. The word Diakonos occurs only seven times in the Septuagint, in reference to those attending to or serving a royal figure. This term is found more frequently during the Persian exile as in Esth 1:10, Esth 2:2 and Esth 6:3 & 5. The Hebrew Scriptures also teach us the concept of liturgical service to God and prophecy of the suffering servant kingship of Jesus the Messiah (Stuhlmueller, 1996, Pages 200-201).

In Acts 6:1-7 we see the first seven who were formally chosen by the Apostles as servants to the church. They were not called deacons at this point, but are generally understood as such by church historians.

> *Acts 6:1-7 Now in those days, when the number of the disciples was multiplying, there arose a complaint against the Hebrews by the Hellenists (Greek Jews), because their widows were neglected in the daily distribution. 2 Then the twelve summoned the*

multitude of the disciples and said, "It is not desirable that we should leave the word of God and serve tables. 3 Therefore, brethren, seek out from among you seven men of good reputation, full of the Holy Spirit and wisdom, whom we may appoint over this business; 4 but we will give ourselves continually to prayer and to the ministry of the word."

5 And the saying pleased the whole multitude. And they chose Stephen, a man full of faith and the Holy Spirit, and Philip, Prochorus, Nicanor, Timon, Parmenas, and Nicolas, a proselyte from Antioch, 6 whom they set before the apostles; and when they had prayed, they laid hands on them.

7 Then the word of God spread, and the number of the disciples multiplied greatly in Jerusalem, and a great many of the priests were obedient to the faith.

In the opening lines of the letter to the Philippians, Paul and Timothy send greetings to the Bishops (Overseers) and Deacons of the Philippian church, as well as to the people there.

> *Philippians 1:1-2 Paul and Timothy, bondservants of Jesus Christ, to all the saints in Christ Jesus who are in Philippi, with the bishops (Overseers) and deacons: 2 Grace to you and peace from God our Father and the Lord Jesus Christ.*

In the Epistle to the Romans, written by St Paul the Apostle somewhere between late 55AD and early 57AD, we see a greeting to a Christian Sister called Phoebe who is also described as a Deacon of the Church. Phoebe has status and honour in the local church and in the mind of St Paul. At this time though, the formal role of Deacons as we know them today had not yet evolved, but clearly, both men and women had these roles of service in the churches. For more on the role of Women in Christian Ministry, please see the chapter on that subject, in Volume Two.

> *Rom 16:1–2: I commend to you Phoebe our sister, who is a servant of the church in*

> Cenchrea, 2 that you may receive her in the Lord in a manner worthy of the saints, and assist her in whatever business she has need of you; for indeed she has been a helper of many and of myself also.

In the book of the Acts of the Apostles chapter 2:17-18 St Peter the Apostle quoting Joel 2:28-29 prophesies that men and women will both be known as the "Servants of God" in "the last days".

> Acts 2:17 *'And it shall come to pass in the last days, says God,*
>
> *That I will pour out of My Spirit on all flesh;*
>
> *Your sons and your daughters shall prophesy,*
>
> *Your young men shall see visions,*
>
> *Your old men shall dream dreams.*
>
> **18 And on MY MENSERVANTS AND ON MY MAIDSERVANTS**
>
> *I will pour out My Spirit in those days;*
>
> *And they shall prophesy.*

1 Timothy 3:1-13 gives us the qualifications for Bishops (Overseers) and Deacons, and therefore for all those called to the formally ordained Priesthood

1 Timothy 3:1-13 This is a faithful saying: If a man desires the position of a bishop, he desires a good work. 2 A bishop then must be blameless, the husband of one wife, temperate, sober-minded, of good behavior, hospitable, able to teach; 3 not given to wine, not violent, not greedy for money, but gentle, not quarrelsome, not covetous; 4 one who rules his own house well, having his children in submission with all reverence 5 (for if a man does not know how to rule his own house, how will he take care of the church of God?); 6 not a novice, lest being puffed up with pride he fall into the same condemnation as the devil. 7 Moreover he must have a good testimony among those who are outside, lest he fall into reproach and the snare of the devil.

8 Likewise deacons must be reverent, not double-tongued, not given to much wine, not greedy for money, 9 holding the mystery of

> *the faith with a pure conscience. 10 But let these also first be tested; then let them serve as deacons, being found blameless. 11 Likewise, their wives must be reverent, not slanderers, temperate, faithful in all things. 12 Let deacons be the husbands of one wife, ruling their children and their own houses well. 13 For those who have served well as deacons obtain for themselves a good standing and great boldness in the faith which is in Christ Jesus.*

The reference to "wives" in the passage above may in fact be a reference to female Deacons which the men who translated the passage did not feel able to state plainly! In our Congress, the Order of Deacons are ordained ministers on the first rung of the priesthood. However, it is not compulsory for a person to be ordained Deacon before being made Priest.

The **Adjutants** who exclusively serve the Bishops are the most senior members of the Order of Deacons in our Congress Ordained Priests and even Bishops can still be Adjutants. For more on the Adjutancy, please see the chapter on this subject in Volume Two.

Priests = an English word derived from the Greek word Presbyteros meaning Elder. In the Congress, Priests are an official rank of leadership. Our view is that while all believers are Priests, not all priests have the same function or operational rank. All ordained Elders are therefore also Priests at the same level of the Presiding Elder who is the "Team Leader" and who usually leads at church services etc. This person chosen from among brothers and sisters however lead as "first among equals" and not as a master over servants. Please see the section on Priesthood in volume two.

Overseers = Honorary Bishops, similar to the Roman Catholic **Monsignor** and permitted to use this title at the discretion of the Presiding Archbishop. This is the first rank of the episcopate and may be granted by the Presiding Archbishop in the context of some ministry responsibilities.

Bishop = The English form of the Greek word Episkopos which means "Overseer" (the person with responsible oversight). Congress Bishops must first be properly ordained priests. They are then selected, elected, appointed and consecrated through the due processes.

Our Bishops trace their Apostolic Succession from Christ through several streams. Please also see the section on Apostolic Succession above for more information on this. Bishops are authorised under proper process to ordain Deacons, Priests and other Bishops, including other Archbishops. In this Congress, Bishops occupy the senior Governmental, Prophetic and Apostolic offices of the church. Each Bishop is assigned by the Presiding Archbishop to a diocese or to other administrative, or diplomatic office as appropriate. Other ranks of the Bishops include: Presiding Bishop (Primate or Archbishop), Ordinary (Diocesan Bishop), Coadjutor, Auxiliary and Suffragan. Please also see the section on becoming an APC Bishop for more on this.

Appointments of others positions such as:

- **Vergers**

- **Lectors**
- **Acolytes**
- **Sub-Deacons and**
- **Others**

Will for now be at the discretion of the Senior Bishop in each nation, in consultation with the Presiding Archbishop, or those to whom they may delegate this function. This Congress does NOT ordain or Consecrate Apostles and or Prophets. We also discourage our members from playing an active part in such events.

Chapter References

Parry, K., Melling, D., Brady, D., Griffith, S., & Healey, J., (Eds), The Blackwell Dictionary of Eastern Christianity, 2000, Blackwell

Stuhlmueller, C., (General Ed), The Collegeville Pastoral Dictionary of Biblical Theology, 1996, Liturgical Press

Ordination/ Consecration of APC Bishops

1Timothy 3.1: This saying is trustworthy: whoever aspires to the office of bishop desires a noble task.

Ordination/ Consecration of APC Bishops:

The Apostolic Pastoral Congress (APC) is a registered association of convergence Charismatic/Pentecostal Bishops, Priests, Pastors and other Clergy. Both the Members' Church Networks and the Congress itself run broadly on Episcopal lines. The APC was founded to provide specialized training and continuing professional development for Christian Ministry & Missions; including Ordination & Ministerial Accreditation.

Clergy in the APC were originally dedicated to serve the United Kingdom and Europe through their Christian Ministry. However we have found that our programs are relevant to and being adapted for many other parts of the world. The Congress offers all members Continuing Professional Development (CPD) Ministry

Training for Clergy from the entry level to the Pastorate or Priesthood, through to the Episcopal offices of the Bishop or General Overseer, according to needs. Clergy training is conducted through St Hadrian's College, based at St John's Rectory, Moston M9 4WE.

The Episcopal Ministry

Bishops in the Congress are normally taken from among the Elders or Presbyters or Priests (which are synonymous among us). They must be consecrated or inducted in due process by the appropriate authorities within the Congress and officially granted their episcopal jurisdiction or other assignments by the Presidium of the Congress. Bishops in the Congress must then therefore, be in the line of succession to the Apostles. Christ is still the Pastor of His Church through the Holy Spirit. Bishops are servants to the churches even as Christ came to serve. It is Christ who still serves the Churches through the Bishops and the Priests even as they surrender themselves to Him.

> *Matthew 20:28 just as the Son of Man did not come to be served, but to serve, and to give His life a ransom for many." (Mark 10:45)*

Bishops are the chief pastors, teachers, administrators and liturgical leaders within their jurisdiction. All Bishops have equal right to administer sacraments, however for order, strength and unity, there are ranks among them. Bishops in this Congress have the major focus of encouraging and facilitating the lifelong (continuing) personal and professional development of the other clergy in the area of their calling. We encourage good teamwork between the Bishop and those who serve God together with them

Bishops in the Congress must meet with other Congress Bishops and clergy in their jurisdiction at least once every year, when apart from learning and Christian fellowship matters of common interest may be discussed and voted on within the Constitution.

Bishops must at all times lead by example in personal holiness and piety, sound family life and be a good public model. They should also be strong defenders of biblically orthodox Christianity and advocates for the churches as well as for the poor and the oppressed; showing Christ by their life and conduct in all things.

Writing to Timothy in the first Epistle of that name, St Paul the Apostle gives clear advice on the qualifications of those who could be chosen from the elders to have oversight (1 Timothy 3:1-7).

> *1 Timothy 3:1-7 This is a faithful saying: If a man desires the position of a bishop, (Episkopos or Overseer) he desires a good work. 2 A bishop then must be blameless, the husband of one wife, temperate, sober-minded, of good behavior, hospitable, able to teach; 3 not given to wine, not violent, not greedy for money, but gentle, not quarrelsome, not covetous; 4 one who rules his own house well, having his children in submission with all reverence 5 (for if a man does not know how to rule his own house, how will he take care of the church of God?); 6 not a novice, lest being puffed up with pride*

> *he fall into the same condemnation as the devil. 7 Moreover he must have a good testimony among those who are outside, lest he fall into reproach and the snare of the devil.*

Bishops in the Congress may represent their jurisdiction in meetings with other clergy in the Congress and sometimes to other Religious, Civic and other Leaders. There is no episcopal infallibility in the Congress. Bishops hold office only as long as they live according to the terms of their appointment and may be reported to the Presidium for not doing so. In extreme cases where the Congress has been brought into serious disrepute, the Presidium may publicly remove Bishops (and Priests or Deacons) from their role in the Congress by writing to them, and serving notice of such removal to all who are known to have dealings with them. The Presiduim may also be called to order by the General Council of Bishops and Clergy meeting during the annual Congress

Ranks of Bishops:

- **Diocesan (Local Geographical)**
- **Suffragan (Assistant to Diocesan)**
- **Overseer (Honorary Appointment)**
- **Archbishop (Wider Geographical)**
- **Presiding Bishop(Similar to Archbishop)**
- **Presiding Archbishop (Metropolitan)**

The Process of Selection and Consecration

The Ordination/ Consecration of Bishops in the APC follows laid down processes and procedures for selection and Ordination/ Consecration.

The APC will normally only consecrate Bishops from among loyal and committed members and leaders of member-Churches of the Christian Way of Life Church Network and/or the Congress. APC Bishops should wherever possible be selected from the area in which they will serve. The APC however also recognizes and receives Bishops into the APC subject to aspects of these protocols as may be appropriate.

Identification of episcopal candidates will usually begin long before vacancies are declared, with prayerful discussion and discernment by the Presidium and potential candidates and/or their sponsoring churches or Senior Bishops. However APC Bishops must have a minimum of ten years pastoral/ministry experience within a recognisable setting. Those the APC selects for elevation to the office of the Bishop, will therefore already have some real proof of practical pastoral ministry or other very strong potentials.

Bishops elect will normally be considered informally at first by a meeting of the APC and/or Colleges of Clergy, or in their ministry setting. Candidates will also be voted for or generally acclaimed in their local church, ministry or network setting and formally proposed in writing by those they have served. These points of the election process are not mutually exclusive.

The nomination to Episcopal Office will be considered by the Presiding Archbishop of the APC and Christian Way of Life Churches who will endeavor to interview them with at least one other experienced clergy. Confidential advice could then be taken from other APC Bishops, other Clergy, trustees and other local church and community leaders etc.

The Bishop's Elect will be formally declared at a meeting of a Clerical College and agreed to by resolution at a general meeting. They will be mentored by a suitable mentor for minimum of 1 year (from any time in this process).

APC and Christian Way of Life Churches Bishops will normally be publicly consecrated by at least 3 duly consecrated Bishops (as in the Eastern Orthodox model) and during an APC liturgical service. The Presiding Archbishop or his successors may be granted dispensation by a quorum of the executive of an APC National or Regional Executive; for consecration by the Archbishop alone (as similar to the South American Roman Catholic model) in peculiar and extenuating circumstances, that the light of the Lord in that Region not be quenched.

In such extenuating circumstances, the Presiding Archbishop (or his successors) may also pass Apostolic Succession directly to candidates, but with the same informed assent of the National/Regional Executive and/or the College of Bishops of the Nation where the new Bishop will be placed.

The consecration of an APC Bishop should be announced publicly in newspapers and/or in the recognized official publication of the area where they are to be placed. In the UK, the date for Ordination/Consecration when set will be Gazetted in the London Gazette not more than 67 and a minimum of 30 days before the consecration service and the copy sent to the Gazette 10 days before the publication date.

Recording of the Consecration

There will normally be three bishops participating in "laying on of hands" when a Bishop is consecrated. Wherever feasible, these three Bishops should each sign the consecration documents or otherwise signify in writing and with their seal that they participated in the consecration. Records must be kept by the Head of Administration, within the APC Presidium, of:

1) Who led each consecration (Presiding Consecrator)

2) Who supported them (Co-Consecrator)

The record then also shows who led the previous consecration of each of the Bishops who conducted this particular consecration, and who the supporting Bishops were for each of their consecrations (see diagram below).

It is then also necessary to show the main line from which the leader of the current consecration we are describing (1) has emerged. That means that we should then show who the main consecrators were for this Bishop also and whoever consecrated them, going back at least three "generations". These historical lines will normally only be for the main (presiding) consecrators. It is not normally necessary to show the lines of the bishops who assisted (co- consecrators) in each consecration going back this far, although they may be mentioned.

Next the record should show the broad history of the line of consecration from which this main line of consecrators comes.

For example, is it Syro-Chaldean or perhaps Russian Orthodox etc. We will often find that there is more than one significant line, and that some of the lines of those who assisted may also be significant, and worthy of a mention.

It is not necessary to show the lines of succession all the way back to Christ in every document. It is however sufficient (and necessary) to show that the newly consecrated bishop is rooted within the main lineage of a recognised episcopal family.

When we find that there is a lack of clarity in the consecration lines of a Bishop or Archbishop, we advise that we will lay hands on them again to establish and perhaps add to the lines of succession they can then claim. We are able to do this in a sensitive way so as not to damage the ministry work that God has already achieved through them.

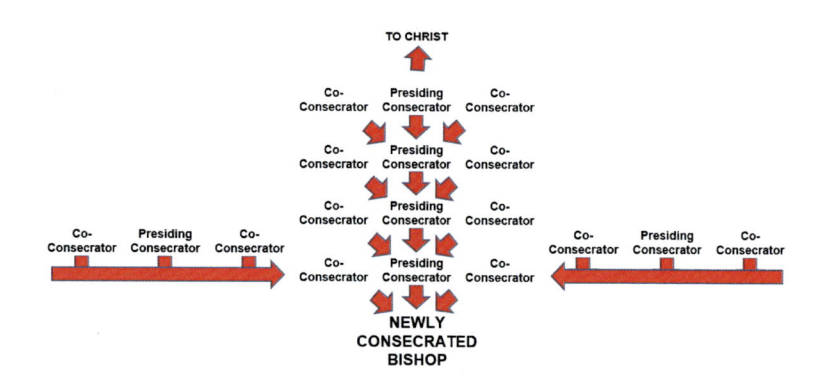

```
                          TO CHRIST
                             ↑
                Co-      Presiding      Co-
            Consecrator  Consecrator  Consecrator
                   ↘         ↓         ↙
                Co-      Presiding      Co-
            Consecrator  Consecrator  Consecrator
                   ↘         ↓         ↙
                Co-      Presiding      Co-
            Consecrator  Consecrator  Consecrator
  Co-    Presiding   Co-      ↘    ↓    ↙      Co-    Presiding   Co-
Consecrator Consecrator Consecrator              Consecrator Consecrator Consecrator
  ──────────────────→   Co-    Presiding   Co-    ←──────────────────
                    Consecrator Consecrator Consecrator
                           ↘      ↓      ↙
                              NEWLY
                           CONSECRATED
                              BISHOP
```

The diagram provided, gives an outline of how the information should be collected and recorded, either before or immediately after the consecration of each new Bishop. The record can also be in tabular, or even narrative form, rather than diagrammatic as suggested here.

Each consecration event should be recorded with the place, date and time that each event occurred, together with the names and official titles of those participating. A copy of the Consecration Certificate, signed by the Presidium and the Head of Administration of the APC, as well as (where possible), all the participating Consecrators, as well as a copy of the lines of Apostolic Succession, should be given to the newly consecrated Bishop as soon as possible after the consecration takes place.

The consecration record may also include other ordinations and consecrations that have taken place for the new Bishop, giving the place, date and time (wherever available) of each event, together with the names and official titles of those participating.

The Roles of the New Bishops

The Annual General Meeting of the APC in the Region/Nation will also duly, resolve that a number of named Bishops will be consecrated, and the date of such consecration agreed. The role of the new Bishops including their geographical, jurisdictional and other aspects of their responsibilities will be published at this time.

These new Bishops will be expected to provide some of the direct assistance to Archbishop Doyé Agama (Presiding Archbishop) and his representative in their Nation/region, as needed in the growing and expanding work of the APC, while also reducing the Archbishop's workload. The Presidium may therefore assign some specific tasks to them, in addition to their local and wider responsibilities.

Bishops and other clergy ordained or consecrated by the Presiding Archbishop or by his representatives, are expected to bring their personal tithe to him, unless granted dispensation by him; and for which dispensation they may apply in writing to the headquarters, stating their reasons.

Each of the Assistant Bishops will go through the laid down APC processes of informal and formal nominations and go through Training/Mentoring with Archbishop Doyé Agama or his designated representative. They will each complete a written proposal for their work over the next three years, set a budget and prepare in other necessary ways for their new role

If successful in passing through all the laid down processes, they may also be nominated to the board of the APC, especially where they can bring particular skills to that role. Once consecrated, APC Bishops will have authority to conduct Ordination/ Consecrations and carry out other recognised ecclesiastical duties within their own ministries and for the APC and more widely with express permission of the Presiding Archbishop, or through a dispensation granted to their National or Regional Presiding Bishop (or Archbishop).

The Qualities of an APC Bishop

The APC Bishop's appointment provides strength and focus for the churches in a given area, or to particular aspects of the churches' mission. The Bishop has a special mandate to preach and teach the Gospel and in so doing to bring the healing of God to every situation.

The APC Bishop should be a focus of unity particularly for their local churches (or other responsibilities) assigned to them, as well as the wider church, and as much as is biblically possible/practical, for the whole community.

He/She should have already occupied some other senior (ordained) church leadership position. Administrative ability is an essential as the Bishop will be expected to manage Church matters at a senior level. The APC Bishop should have (and be developing) their mediation skills, including intercession, intervention, arbitration, negotiation and reconciliation

They should have good communication skills, be a good and confident public speaker; and be familiar with the use of the modern digital media including social media and be comfortable dealing with the press and the public. The Bishop must have a good understanding of and ability to teach on Christian Sacraments, Liturgy and Vestments.

The Bishop is appointed to serve the clergy and the people of the church and not to be served by them. The Bishop is appointed to serve the wider church and the community as well as their own church(es). As a servant leader, the Bishop must be of good character; charismatic and also approachable; and having empathy with others according to 1Tim 3. The Bishop Elect must also be:

- A good Pastor of souls

    John 21:15-17 So when they had eaten breakfast, Jesus said to Simon Peter, "Simon, son of Jonah, do you love Me more than these?"

    He said to Him, "Yes, Lord; You know that I love You."

    He said to him, "Feed My lambs."

    16 He said to him again a second time, "Simon, son of Jonah, do you love Me?"

    He said to Him, "Yes, Lord; You know that I love You."

    He said to him, "Tend My sheep."

    17 He said to him the third time, "Simon, son of Jonah, do you love Me?" Peter was grieved because He said to him the third time, "Do you love Me?"

And he said to Him, "Lord, You know all things; You know that I love You."

Jesus said to him, "Feed My sheep.

Matthew 28:19 Go therefore and make disciples of all the nations, baptizing them in the name of the Father and of the Son and of the Holy Spirit

1 Timothy 4:6-11 If you instruct the brethren in these things, you will be a good minister of Jesus Christ, nourished in the words of faith and of the good doctrine which you have carefully followed. 7 But reject profane and old wives' fables, and exercise yourself toward godliness. 8 For bodily exercise profits a little, but godliness is profitable for all things, having promise of the life that now is and of that which is to come. 9 This is a faithful saying and worthy of all acceptance. 10 For to this end we both labor and suffer reproach, because we trust in the living God, who is the Savior of all men, especially of

> those who believe. 11 These things command and teach.

- A sound teacher of the Pentecostal Christian Faith

    > Titus 1:5-11 For this reason I left you in Crete, that you should set in order the things that are lacking, and appoint elders in every city as I commanded you— 6 if a man is blameless, the husband of one wife, having faithful children not accused of dissipation or insubordination. 7 For a bishop (Episkopos or Overseer) must be blameless, as a steward of God, not self-willed, not quick-tempered, not given to wine, not violent, not greedy for money, 8 but hospitable, a lover of what is good, sober-minded, just, holy, self-controlled, 9 holding fast the faithful word as he has been taught, that he may be able, by sound doctrine, both to exhort and convict those who contradict. 10 For there are many insubordinate, both idle talkers and deceivers,

especially those of the circumcision, 11 whose mouths must be stopped, who subvert whole households, teaching things which they ought not, for the sake of dishonest gain.

- Of a good reputation

    1 Timothy 3:2 A bishop then must be blameless, the husband of one wife, temperate, sober-minded, of good behavior, hospitable, able to teach;

- Prudent and of good judgement Tit 1:7
- Cool and stable tempered

    1 Timothy 3:3 not given to wine, not violent, not greedy for money, but gentle, not quarrelsome, not covetous;

- Loyal and obedient to authority

    Romans 13:1 Let every soul be subject to the governing authorities. For there is no authority except from God, and the authorities that exist are appointed by God.

- Committed to personal spiritual and intellectual development, a student of good theological education

    2 Timothy 2:15 Be diligent to present yourself approved to God, a worker who does not need to be ashamed, rightly dividing the word of truth.

    2 Timothy 3:16 All Scripture is given by inspiration of God, and is profitable for doctrine, for reproof, for correction, for instruction in righteousness,

- A manager with administrative acumen Acts 6:1-7

- Committed to a Biblical family life 1Tim 3: 2

The APC Bishop must have fulfilled the conditions of a Deacon. The Bishop should also be an evangelist, committed to mission and ministry, with some apostolic aspects to their own call and ministry. They must be faithful to the biblical apostolic message (the Kerygma of the Apostles) and be submitted to scriptural apostolic authority. They should be fervent worshippers of God

Bishops, like all other clergy are the catalysts, facilitators and enablers of the lay people who do the work of the church through evangelising their friends neighbors and work colleagues; as well as service to the community. The APC Bishop must be committed to the raising up of new generations of clergy and laity to continue the work of God's Kingdom.

The bishop must defend the biblical Christian faith against revisionist theories and outright heresies. (Jude 3) They are only able to hold others accountable if they have lived a Godly life themselves. (Titus 1:9-11, 2:1)

> *Titus 1:9-11 holding fast the faithful word as he has been taught, that he may be able, by sound doctrine, both to exhort and convict those who contradict. 10 For there are many insubordinate, both idle talkers and deceivers, especially those of the circumcision, 11 whose mouths must be stopped, who subvert whole*

> *households, teaching things which they ought not, for the sake of dishonest gain.*

As a high profile representative of the church, the APC Bishop must be and be seen to be living a good moral life. They must have a deep personal spirituality as well as sufficient intellectual ability for this role. The Bishop must have a disciplined life of personal holiness, built through bible study, prayer and fasting.

They should be quiet, sober, respectable and hospitable, with a good family life. (1 Tim. 3:2-7) As a public and private example of what we believe to be the Biblical ideal/standard, APC Bishops should be in a heterosexual, monogamous marriage for life.

> *1 Timothy 3:2-7 A bishop then must be blameless, the husband of one wife, temperate, sober-minded, of good behavior, hospitable, able to teach; 3 not given to wine, not violent, not greedy for money, but gentle, not quarrelsome, not covetous; 4 one who rules his own house well, having his children in submission with all reverence 5 (for if a*

> *man does not know how to rule his own house, how will he take care of the church of God?); 6 not a novice, lest being puffed up with pride he fall into the same condemnation as the devil. 7 Moreover he must have a good testimony among those who are outside, lest he fall into reproach and the snare of the devil.*

Bishops must have a relatively high work-rate/ethic without losing focus or balance in their personal life. The role of the Bishop can be stressful and lonely, sometimes requiring separation from legitimate pleasure and comfort, much travel, and long work hours etc. The Bishop must therefore be willing to be accountable to those above them as well as to those under their authority. They should be of sound enough health for the role.

Their teaching should be informed by scripture, tradition and reason, but with the Bible as the final arbiter of truth. They must be clear in their own Christian conviction, while respecting the views of other churches, having a good understanding of the historic Christian faith, and the contemporary expression of this heritage in 21st Century relevance. In addition the APC Bishop should be:

- Prepared to engage with local and central government as well as with other statutory and other Voluntary and Community Service (VCS) providers in the area of their deployment

- Prepared to engage to an extent with other denominations and other faith leaders in the area of their deployment

- Able to grasp and exercise the opportunities God gives for their prophetic, and evangelistic role in society

Chapter References

http://www.gotquestions.org

http://orthodoxwiki.org/Bishop

http://www.newadvent.org/cathen/

The Noble Communion and Holy Apostolic Order of St Hadrian of Canterbury

Our "sister organisation" is the Order of Saint Hadrian of Canterbury. St Hadrian (or Adrian) of Canterbury (otherwise known as St Hadrian the African), was born in a Greek speaking part of Cyrenaica in Libya around AD 635. Arriving in Naples as a refugee from the Arab invasions of the 7th century, he rose to become an Abbot first at Nisida and then of St. Augustine's Abbey at Canterbury.

In AD 668, St Hadrian declined appointment by Pope Vitalian as Archbishop to the vacant See of Canterbury. St Hadrian recommended his good friend St. Theodorus (Theodore) of Tarsus to become the Archbishop; and went on to serve as St Theodore as an assistant and adviser. As Abbot of the leading Seminary in England at that time, St Hadrian also became a mentor to many principal churchmen. He died on 9th January AD 710 at Canterbury. His feast continues on that day.

The Order of St Hadrian was originally founded by Archbishop Doyé Agama as a non-chivalric, Pentecostal Christian and Educational Order based in the United Kingdom. Members of this Religious Order pledge to uphold the memory of St Hadrian, through his tenets of exemplary humility, excellence in service; and training up new generations to serve the church and community.

Works of the Order:

1. The Order works ecumenically to research and publicize the contributions of ancient and contemporary Christians and churches from outside Europe to the Christian Religion.

2. The Order introduces some aspects of Monastic Prayer Life back into modern churches, especially the Black Pentecostals

3. The Order supports the training of the Congress through St Hadrian's College Manchester, England.

4. The Order particularly recognises outstanding community service by Christians from Black and other heritage in the UK and beyond.

5. The Order especially recognises the contributions of others to the minority ethnic Christian European Diaspora and the nations of the origins of that Diaspora.

6. The Order carries out charitable works in line with the ethos of the Order.

7. January 9th each year is the main "Feast Day" of The Order.

8. Awards of the Order are given each October, but can be given at other times.

Membership and the Rule of the Order:

The Senior Abbot (currently Archbishop Doyé T. Agama) is the Head of the Order under Christ for as long as he lives a biblical life. In the event of his demise or incapacitation, the members of the order shall vote for no more than 3 persons; to choose one as the new Abbot. Each Clergy member of the Order shall have two votes, and lay members only one vote. In the event of a tie or other dispute, the Grand Patron shall take a final decision in consultation with the Board of Patrons.

The headquarters of the Order shall be in Canterbury in England (this is still pending) with the second ranking Abbey in the North West of England. Abbeys, Priories and Volunteer Associations shall be established according to due process in any country of the world and shall bear spiritual allegiance under Jesus Christ, to the Senior Abbot and to the Grand Patron; in all matters of the Order.

Members of The Order are committed to support each other towards stability and positive growth of community through Biblical Family Life, Local Church Life, and Business Enterprise. This is to be achieved through the basic disciplines of The Order which are Obedience to Christian Scripture, Holiness, Study,

Prayer, Worship and Community Service. Membership of this Order shall be Apostolic-Vocational. Members of The Order are particularly called to work for the building of the Christian Churches and community.

Membership in the Apostolic Order of Saint Hadrian of Canterbury is open to men and women who are recommended by and are in good standing as members of member churches of the Apostolic Pastoral Congress, the Christian Way of Life Churches, or churches duly recognised by them; and others acceptable to The Order. A number of Members of the order are also Patrons of the Order.

Nominations for Membership of the Order can be sent by post to: The Apostolic Order of St Hadrian of Canterbury, St John's Rectory, Railton Terrace, Moston, Manchester M9 4WE England, or Email: doye[at]hotmail.com.

The Chivalric Ranks of the Order:

Archbishop J Delano Ellis II GCHC, or his designated Episcopal successors shall have a primary Jurisdiction for this Order in the USA. Archbishop Doyé Teido Agama GCHC, and his designated Episcopal successors as duly selected as Senior Abbot, shall have a Jurisdiction for Europe, Africa, Asia and Oceania. These jurisdictions are not exclusive. In all Liturgical and Civic Protocol, Archbishop Ellis shall however have the precedence, followed by Archbishop Doyé Agama.

Archbishop Ellis and Archbishop Agama shall jointly appoint the International Executive Boards for this Order, and the Boards shall be answerable to them. Archbishop Ellis or Archbishop Agama may select the recipients of the Honours conferred by this Order, on the advice of their Colleges of Bishops and Clergy.

His Imperial Highness Prince Ermias Sahle-Selassie Haile-Selassie GCHC, President of the Crown Council of Ethiopia is the Grand Patron of the Apostolic Order of St Hadrian of Canterbury (Imperial Patronage was granted to this modern Order on 6th May 2010). With the granting of Imperial Patronage the Order has been reviewed in line with ancient chivalric tradition.

THE CROWN COUNCIL OF ETHIOPIA
የኢ ትዮጵያ ዘውድ ምክር ቤት

OFFICE OF THE PRESIDENT

PO BOX 320608, ALEXANDRIA, VIRGINIA 22320, UNITED STATES OF AMERICA.

Alexandria, Virginia: May 6, 2010

The Very Reverend Bishop (Dr) Doyé T. Agama
President of the Apostolic Order of St Hadrian of Canterbury
St. John's Rectory
Railton Terrace
Moston, Manchester M9 4WE
UNITED KINGDOM.

My Dear Bishop Dr Agama:

It is with great pleasure that we accept the Honour and Responsibility of providing Imperial Patronage to The Apostolic Order of St. Hadrian of Canterbury, and to assist in its ecumenical work to help unite, and further the cause of cooperation among, the Christian churches. The example of Saint Hadrian of Canterbury is a rallying point for Christians around the world, as well as a symbol of the unity of faith of African and European Christians.

We look forward to working closely with you, and the Order, in this worthy endeavour.

Yours sincerely,

His Imperial Highness
Prince Ermias Sahle-Selassie Haile-Selassie,
President, The Crown Council of Ethiopia.

HONOURS IN THE APOSTOLIC ORDER OF ST HADRIAN OF CANTERBURY INCLUDE THE FOLLOWING RANKS:

1. Neophyte (Member)
2. Associate Fellow (Member (H))
3. Fellow (Officer)
4. Fellow of the International Entrepreneurial Circle (Officer (H))
5. Senior Fellow (Commander)
6. Distinguished Fellow (Knight/Dame)
7. Grand Companion (Knight/Dame (H))
8. Life Fellow (Knight/Dame Commander)
9. Patron (Knight/Dame Commander (H))
10. Grand Cross or Grand Cordon(Knight/Dame Grand Cross)

PATRONS OF THE ORDER:

Current Patrons of the Apostolic Order of St Hadrian of Canterbury are: Archbishop J. Delano Ellis II

(Metropolitan, Joint College of Afro-American Pentecostal Bishops) (Co-Founder, Patron & Life Fellow 2008), Archbishop Doyé Agama Presidium of The Apostolic Pastoral Congress & The Christian Way of Life Churches (Founder, Patron & Life Fellow, & the First Abbot of the Order 2008), Bishop Nigel McCulloch (Church of England, Bishop Emeritus of Manchester) (Patron & Life Fellow 2009), Bishop David Hawkins (Church of England, Bishop Emeritus of Barking) (Patron & Distinguished Fellow Emeritus 2009), Bishop Chris Edmondson (Church of England, Bishop of Bolton) (Patron and Senior Fellow 2009), Bishop Angaelos (General Bishop of the Coptic Orthodox Church of Alexandria, Patron & Senior Fellow 2010).

Chapter references

http://en.wikipedia.org/wiki/Adrian_of_Canterbury

https://apostolicpastors.info/order-of-st-hadrian

http://en.wikipedia.org/wiki/Apostolic_Pastoral_Congress#The_Order_of_St_Hadrian_of_Canterbury